Dear Sibelius

Statue of the young Sibelius in Sibelius Park, Hämeenlinna

Dear Sibelius
Letter from a Junky

Marshall Walker

Kennedy & Boyd
an imprint of
Zeticula
57 St Vincent Crescent
Glasgow
G3 8NQ
Scotland

http://www.kennedyandboyd.co.uk
admin@kennedyandboyd.co.uk

First published in 2008
Text Copyright © Marshall Walker 2008
Photographs © Marshall Walker 2008 except
for those of Elliot Junction (pages 67 and 68)
courtesy of the Angus Council, Angus Cultural
Services,
and that of Ian Whyte, (page 110) courtesy of BBC
Scottish Symphony Orchestra .

ISBN-13 978 1 904999 68 3
ISBN-10   1 904999 68 9

Para Cláudia,
minha música sempre

Milford Sound, Fjordland

'Obscurely yet most surely called to praise'

(Richard Wilbur, 'Praise in Summer')

For me, a certain sign of quality or
class in art is that when I read, see or
listen to something, I suddenly get an
acute, clear feeling that somebody's
formulated something which I've
experienced or thought; exactly the
same thing but with the help of a better
sentence or better visual arrangement
or better composition of sounds than
I could ever have imagined. Or, for a
moment, gave me a sense of beauty, joy
or something like that.

(Krzysztof Kieslowski)

'If I should ever die, God forbid, let this be
my epitaph: "The only proof he needed
for the existence of God was music"'.

(Kurt Vonnegut)

Seagulls off Oban

Contents

List of Illustrations

I have a good mind
take into my head
to start off singing
begin reciting
reeling off a tale of kin
and singing a tale of kind.

(*Kalevala*, Rune 1)

Dear Sibelius,

You won't be surprised that I went to Koli. Any devotee of your Karelia music might do the same. But I was looking for the landscape of your Fourth Symphony. It's the most cryptic and personal of the seven symphonies you called your 'confessions of faith', so I wanted to be where you were when it began to sound in your mind.

It's not so hard to reach Koli now as it must have been in your time. Five hours by train north-east from Helsinki to Joensuu, gateway to the Karelia, through tunnels of forest with glimpses of farms and lakes through gaps in the long green walls. Then two more climbing and twisting hours by local bus. I don't know how you got there in September 1909, but you said that the place was one of your 'life's greatest experiences'. I'm sure that when you're not at 'Ainola', your home near Helsinki for over fifty years, you're at Koli still, 'rolled round in earth's diurnal course' with Koli Mountain and mighty Lake Pielinen.

I'm writing in time for your birthday. You'll be 143 on the 8th of December 2008. We saluted the fiftieth anniversary of your death on 20th September last year, but I'd rather mark your next birthday. It would have been neater if I'd written for your centennial in 1965, but I've only recently managed to make the trip to Koli. So it just happens that now is the time I feel I can try to write you a proper letter.

Why you? After all, Beethoven has been a life-long familiar, and Brahms and Dvorak, Elgar and Prokofiev. But you've been a comrade, a point of reference, an addiction. So this is a letter from a junky. You went in so deep, so early.

1

1. Fog and the island

Everything was foggy at the beginning. That was a long time before you came down from Finland to the music room of a Scottish school. I was twelve when you came. You were eighty-four, Finland's national treasure. 'Sibelius to the rescue', I've often thought. All my life since then I've wanted to thank you.

You couldn't clear the fog, but you gave me a way of living in it. The lenses of my glasses were as thick as milk-bottle bottoms. My eyes looked tiny through them from the other side, like a pig's. The frames had to be thick too, to carry the weight of the lenses. If I wasn't 'Piggy' to the boys in my class I was 'Specky' or 'Four Eyes' when I stumbled into chairs and bumped into desks. The glasses hardly seemed worth the ridicule, they delivered so little of the world.

The English teacher was acid. He was telling us how to deduce character from appearance.

'For example', he said, 'I distrust a person who wears spectacles with heavy frames'.

The class sniggered. Heads turned to stare at me. I kept my eyes down on the desk, but in the distortion of my peripheral vision their faces were distended pale balloons of derision.

'An attempt to add an air of distinction to an otherwise featureless face', the English teacher said, driving the nail home. You didn't need to see the smirk on his face. It was audible.

How could someone who taught poetry be cruel like that? It was confusing, like the distance between Wagner's anti-Semitism and the tenderness of the *Siegfried Idyll* or the love of Siegmund and Sieglinde in *Die Walküre*. How I loved my 12 inch shellac record of the 'Magic Fire Music' in an orchestral arrangement by Stokowski and the Philadelphia

Orchestra, the tongues of flame, Wotan's woebegone fatherhood and the peerless warrior woman on her rock. A Christmas present from my father. But was love reserved for brawny Teutons, members of the master race? How could a man who understood passionate love utter such racist hatred, calling *Der Jude* 'the plastic demon of the decay of humanity'? How would Wagner have been judged at Nuremberg, the Nazis' *Götterdämmerung*? Would they have let him off because he wrote good tunes? How could he win the advocacy, even the devotion of Jewish Mahler, Bruno Walter, Klemperer, Solti, Barenboim? Or did they know he later regretted the dirty nineteenth-century orthodoxy of his anti-Semitism?

What about the overture to *Die Meistersinger* blaring from the death camps' loudspeakers while victims of the Final Solution limped to the gas chambers, the evocation of Nazi night-time parades and rallies in *Siegfried's Rhine Journey* and Hagen's steerhorn summons to the Gibichung, the posse of Leni Riefenstahls in *The Ride of the Valkyries*? No doubt about it, *The Ring of the Nibelung* is replete with Hitler's favourite themes: heroism (Siegmund, Siegfried and Brünnhilde), blood (lots), race (Nibelung dwarfs versus cheating gods; heroes versus dwarfs, a dragon and Gibichung).

What did you make of all that, Sibelius? As a young composer you were in some danger of falling under Wagner's spell like so many of your contemporaries. Weren't the *liebestod*s of *Der Fliegende Holländer*, *Der Ring des Nibelungen* and *Tristan und Isolde* expressions of the breast-beating romanticism of German nationalism and the Reich's poisoning seductions? It doesn't help to say, 'Just concentrate on the music or the poetry and forget the man'. Not with this man and not with my English teacher.

4

Later on there could be choice. My *Ring* could be about the triumph of love over lust for power. Hitler lost, so does power when the ring is returned to the Rhinemaidens out of the love of Brünnhilde and Siegfried as Valhalla and the *Reich* of capitalist Führer Wotan combust. It's a fable we can't get enough of even now (can we, Bush, Ahmadinejad, Osama, Putin?) Yes, later I could resolve to be sophisticated and discriminating about inconsistent things, like Mahler, Barenboim and the rest. But that's not an option when you're eleven, remembering the War and the searing Pathé newsreels of the death camps' skeletal surviving Jews. The English writer, William Empson, copes with this kind of dilemma when he says, 'life involves maintaining oneself between contradictions that can't be solved by analysis'. Your wisest music maintains itself exactly there. My English teacher was somewhere else.

People were blurs with voices and smells, gradually taking on detail as ophthalmic fashion prescribed lenses with fuller correction. I knew how my parents looked in photographs, because I could hold the brown-paged albums at the end of my nose, and I knew what their hands looked like from when my mother applied sticking-plaster to a cut and from my father's regular clipping of my fingernails. He insisted on short back and sides for hair and close to the quick for nails. That was how to be masculine. He'd clip a finger and hold it up to me to see what a real boy's nails should look like. I knew more about what Granny and my colony of aunts looked like because they fussed over me more than my parents did, so I saw them up close quite often.

At the beginning you don't know your world is foggier than other people's. You wonder why everyone else navigates with more confidence about where and how things are. You tend to feel stupid. Remember you once said you thought of becoming an idiot? Well, I often thought I'd been born one, an oafish oxymoron, a spectator who couldn't see.

The fog brought intimacy with pavements. I fell on them from assorted heights, walking, running or climbing.

'Look where you're going', my parents said.

At the centre of the fog was a semi-detached house on Glasgow's south side. The air was full of war.

Sibelius, you were only two when your father died and you were snatched with your mother and sister out of your first home in the town of Hämeenlinna. I was two as well when Hitler dislodged my mother and father and me from a tenement flat at Anniesland Cross. That's in the West End of Glasgow. The building was on the Luftwaffe's flight-path to the River Clyde where there were shipyards to be bombed. It was safer on the south side of the river. When we went there we had, as they said, 'evacuated'. This led to some bewilderment when the doctor asked if I'd had 'a good evacuation'. The suburb was called 'Whitecraigs'. That sounded posh enough to be safe. The city flat was sub-let to an elegant Polish doctor and his beautiful olive-skinned wife. Throughout the war the doctor performed illegal abortions on our dining-room table. The beautiful wife kennelled her under-exercised Alsatian in my bedroom. You could say that my bedroom carpet was a casualty of war.

Well-to-do friends lent us the house on the south side and evacuated themselves even further away from Hitler. This didn't seem fair because it meant that there were degrees of safety unequally available. The Polish doctor and his beautiful wife got a bright little flat with a view of the Old Kilpatrick Hills, but

The flat at Anniesland Cross, top left

a bomb could fall on them. We weren't as safe as we could have been because there was the much safer place my parents' friends had gone to. Hitler was everyone's enemy, so why didn't everyone go together to the safest place of all? And where was that? The safer place the friends had gone to was Prestwick in Ayrshire, by the sea. That meant that they were dodging Hitler and having a seaside holiday. How could they have a holiday when Hitler was trying to kill us?

'You'll understand later,' said my father.

Holding my hand on the way home from shopping, my mother stopped and looked up at the sky. I saw nothing, but heard the plane's engines.

'You see that dot in the sky?' said my mother.

'Yes,' I said because I knew I was expected to.

'That's a German reconnaissance plane,' my mother said.

'What's reconnaissance?'

'Looking around.'

'Can it see us?'

'We'd better take the shopping inside. Look where you're going.'

***

Dear Sibelius, you've been my companion for so long that I've just been surprised to realize you didn't know about all this. I know your country sided with Germany and I understand that this wasn't because you supported Hitler but because Finland couldn't go along with Stalin. Russia had hammered your people for generations. Sometimes it's been quite hard for Scotland to go along with England for similar reasons. I know the war depressed you but I'm glad that you turned down Britain's offer of asylum. You stayed Finnish, true to your earth and light and swans and cranes. There's heartfelt patriotism in your greatest hit, *Finlandia*, originally called *Finland Awakes*. 'Pure inspiration', you called it. With the music that became the first set of your *Scènes Historiques* you wrote it for a series of tableaux presented in Helsinki's Swedish Theatre in 1899, the year the Tsar took away your country's freedom of speech. A gala occasion. The authorities thought it was in aid of a Press Pension Fund, but it was really a show of Finnish opposition to Imperial Russia. It quickly became Finland's true national anthem and asserted the country's link with classical music.

What a jump from that new ignition of national pride to the plum-label 78 rpm record I bought in Glasgow as a twelve-year-old novice Sibelian. Daring a solo tram journey to the downtown record shop and reciting the catalogue number. Admiring the salesgirl's quizzical eyebrows when I leaned into her across the counter to confide your name.

'Jean Sibelius'.

'Is he a singer?'

'Sort of,' I said, falling in love.

She handed me the record in its cardboard sleeve, plucked from shelves she visited only for weird people who didn't want Bing Crosby or the Andrews Sisters. This was John Barbirolli and the Hallé Orchestra of Manchester. Six shillings and tenpence: a birthday postal order plus accumulated pocket money.

'Fancy coming to listen to it with me?' I said to the girl.

'Awa' tae yer bed for a month,' she said, taking my money. 'Yer Granny's a cowboy'.

Home on the tram, holding the record to my chest

away from the press of other passengers, to watch the pick-up of the record player ride the grooves of clarion brass. Schoolboy adrenalin pumping with the drums and cymbals. Then astonishment when I found a hymn. It was the tune we sang in blazered conformity at school prayers. The hymn was horrible:

Be still, my soul: the Lord is on your side;
bear patiently the cross of grief and pain;
leave to your God to order and provide;
in every change he faithful will remain.

No. Your music couldn't mean this. I had no awareness of a post-war Lord and even less sense of whose side he might be on. The words were a deformity imposed on music which had nothing to do with acceptance of grief and pain. It was about proud identity and a hopeful vision of the future. You were fired by the surge of your people for independence, freedom from tsarist oppression. But the hymn got worse:

Be still, my soul: for Jesus can repay
from his own fullness all he takes away.

So the Lord is on my side, yet his Jesus takes away. But this is a reason for thanksgiving because Jesus also can repay everything if he feels like it. The Church's doubletalk. If Jesus was on my side he wouldn't take away in the first place. In the school hall I swayed to your music in dreamy, rhythmic happiness but even then hated the words.

Vindication of my revulsion from the words of the hymn came later when I discovered the patriotic verses you approved for your mixed-choir arrangement of the *Finlandia Anthem*:

10

O Finland, see, thy day is dawning,
The threat of night is banished away;
And the lark sings in the morning
As if the vault of heaven did ring.
The splendour of morning has conquered the
power of night,
The day is dawning, O fatherland.

If patriotism is the last refuge of a scoundrel, well, better a scoundrel than a wimp.

***

The house on the south side didn't feel safe for long. This was partly because of the fog. I tripped on the front doorstep, split my forehead and sat in the doctor's surgery holding cotton wool to the gash. The doctor's rimless glasses, the cavernous menace of his panelled room and the gleaming steel dishes in which instruments for my repair were sterilized told me I had been wickedly clumsy and would be systematically punished by new, sophisticated levels of pain.

But there was more to it than the fog. There was my father's moustache.

It was a dark smudge below his nose. Hitler had one too, a rectangle of coal under his greasy quiff. Why did my father decorate himself with an emblem of the monster? And later, from the front row of the picture house, squinching my eyes into slits to make them telescopic, why did Charlie Chaplin? He had to be a good person, didn't he? He made me laugh and cry for the balletic mischief and poignancy of the tramp. Why did he wear the same sinister growth on his lip? When the air-raid siren wailed its warning a mile and a half away, was it to announce the approach of a Nazi gang coming to get me? Would there be torture, unimaginably worse than the doctor's surgery? Was the gang of terror – Hitler, my father and Charlie Chaplin – linked by the code of their moustaches?

Your ample young-man's moustache, Sibelius, when you were thirty, working on *Four Legends from the Kalevala*, lacked this clipped intimidation. But I was easier with Karsh of Ottawa's portraits of a magisterial shaven-headed man in a white suit. Karsh remembered 'a happy man full of infectious laughter'. He probably knew about your time as hell-raiser, the wild man of *Kullervo*, the First Symphony, *Finlandia* and *En Saga*. You loved *haute cuisine*, fine wine, leisurely conversation, whisky, cigars and sharp clothes. You were a man for a binge, though severity, if not austerity, was always fundamental to your aesthetic. Karsh's photographs have encouraged us to visualize you as someone large, old and grim, the man who once said to a pupil, 'When we see these granite rocks we know why we can treat the orchestra as we do'. A man carved from rock, introspective, austerely remote, you seemed to be a solitary even among your family at 'Ainola', someone from the world of ice and snow presided over by Tapio, the bleak god of your symphonic poem, *Tapiola*.

The air-raid siren said we might be going to die tonight. My mother was clever about that.

'Oh, listen, there's our friend again, Softy the Siren', she said.

It worked up to a point. When the doleful noise sent me burrowing under the bedclothes I'd say out loud, 'There goes old Softy'. But when Softy sounded the 'All Clear' I half expected to emerge from my quilted shelter to find Hitler, my father and Charlie Chaplin standing over the bed with intricate Gestapo plans for my immediate future.

12

13

'When we see these granite rocks we know why we can treat the orchestra as we do'

Roger was the boy next door. He was my own age and we usually managed to be friends, though he looked down on me because I was evacuated and bumped into things. I condescended to him because he wasn't and didn't. He was having too easy a war, I thought. Roger's house had high white rough-cast gateposts with flat tops about a metre square. A fir tree grew close enough to one of the gateposts for its branches to make a convenient ladder. Roger climbed the branches and stepped from the tree to the gatepost top. Here he surveyed the street and kept an eye open for Germans.

'You can come up if you want', he'd say, pretending not to care.

I always went up, scratching hands and face in the tree's dark centre, swinging out towards the blur that was Roger on his concrete pedestal. After a moment's exaltation I'd step over the unseen edge. When I'd picked myself up from the slap of the pavement and the smell of warm tar – for the gatepost was a summer ploy – I'd take the shame home. My mother would speak calmly.

'I'll run you a bath', she'd say.

After the bath I comforted myself with the gramophone which lived in a corner of the dining room. This was where we gathered, facing the wireless in a crescent of straight-backed chairs to laugh resolutely at the comedian, Tommy Handley in *ITMA*, or hear about the war from Mr Churchill. The gramophone's cabinet was made of walnut and smelled of felt and varnish. Inside the lid was a miniature of Francis Barraud's 'His Master's Voice' and 'Nipper' became my favourite dog for ever. The first favourite record was Paul Robeson singing 'Ol' Man River'. Aching

14

from the fall, warm from the bath, I wound up the motor, placed the ten-inch record on the turntable and swung in the shiny nickel-plated tone arm to bring sound-box and needle down to the run-in groove. In a second the magic would happen again. At my command the wise genie, my familiar, would bring me his sympathy through the gramophone's wooden grille:

> *You and me, we sweat and strain,*
> *Body all achin' and racked with pain.*
> *'Tote that barge!', 'Lift that bale!'*
> *You get a little drunk and you land in jail.*
>
> *I get weary and sick of tryin',*
> *I'm tired of livin' and scared of dyin',*
> *But ol' man river, he just keeps rollin' along.*

Robeson knew what it was like all right; you could count on him. He knew about the fall from the gatepost, body all aching. He knew about being weary and sick of the fog. Getting a row for bumping into things was the same as landing in jail. He knew about being scared of dying, which I was whenever I saw my elders look up at the sky or Softy the siren announced the end of the world. But he also knew about the river which, godlike, would prevail in spite of Hitler. Later this became the recognizable truth at the beginning of T.S. Eliot's 'The Dry Salvages':

> *I do not know much about gods; but I think*
>   *that the river*
> *Is a strong brown god...*

They said Robeson was a Negro, more black than brown, but that was close enough. He was God in the gramophone, the river's voice, my unfailing friend.

15

But I failed him, because of the fog. After another fall from the gatepost and another bath, I couldn't find the record in its usual place, leaning with others against the wall in the corner beside the gramophone. In frustration I sank to a chair and sat on 'Ol' Man River'. First came the obscure crack, then the horror of shellac fragments. It was my first true loss, first taste of death. I had killed the river and violated the genie. I'd destroyed music and the voice of understanding. I had killed God. Hitler would kill me. My father would help him and Charlie Chaplin would laugh and dance. I had brought disgrace on my family and Softy would never sound the 'All Clear' again.

I told my mother, words mangled by tears.
'It was an accident', she said and withdrew into adult concerns.

There was no place for a boy's broken god in the wartime economy. We were waiting to be gassed. Maybe that's why I thought germs and Germans were the same. Both infected the air. I had a Mickey Mouse gas mask. The rubber smell was sickening. The grown-ups talked mostly about the gas on Sunday afternoon when the week-end had reached its doldrums. I sometimes thought they wished it would come.

Some grown-ups sounded quite jolly when they sang the song about the rabbit.

Run, rabbit, run rabbit, run, run, run,
Don't give the farmer his fun, fun, fun,
He'll get by without his rabbit pie,
So run, rabbit, run, rabbit, run, run, run.

I was glad the grown-ups were on the rabbit's side, but suddenly the rabbit turned into Hitler.

17

Dunollie Castle, near Oban

Run, Adolf, run Adolf, run, run, run
Look what you've been gone and done, done,
  done.
We will knock the stuffing out of you;
Field Marshal Goering and Goebbels too.

You'll lose your place in the sun, sun sun;
Soon, you poor dog, you'll get none, none,
  none.
You will flop with Herr Von Ribbentrop,
So Run, Adolf, run Adolf, run, run, run.

How could Hitler be a rabbit, then a dog? He was more like the farmer with the gun. The other people in the song with ugly names probably had guns as well. And if the grown-ups were so sure they could knock the stuffing out of Hitler and his nasty friends why were so many of them evacuated and scared of German planes and bombs and poison gas?

'Don't ask so many questions', said my father.

***

But there was time for holidays and I began to know the island of Lismore. It became my paradise as yours was Lovisa, the seafaring town north-east of Helsinki, where you stayed with your grandmother during school holidays, exploring the archipelago. On sailing trips you'd stand in the prow of the boat and extemporize to the waves on your violin. Wherever you were you carried Lovisa with you. Similarly, Lismore took possession of me, becoming my 'island that likes to be visited', like the faery island J. M. Barrie made up for his other-worldly heroine in *Mary Rose*. Not that it tempted me to vanish like Barrie's waifish Mary, though it was always a wrench to leave

19

Lismore pier

it when the holiday was over and we were pulled back to the mainland by my father's job and the new school term.

Lismore is a splinter of land in the sea of Loch Linnhe in Argyllshire. It lies off Port Appin to the north, seven miles from the market town of Oban to the south. The Gaelic name means 'Great Garden'. It sits in the middle of a landscape made by the long-extinct volcano whose core now comprises Ben More, the highest peak on the island of Mull. A low-lying island, its chief marvel, ribbed by underlying folds of limestone, is its highest point, the Bàrr Mòr ('Big Top'), a modest 417 feet. When you're up there you can see almost the whole Great Glen of Scotland. You can imagine sunlight flashing on the oars of Vikings – perhaps a forebear of yours among them, Sibelius – and relish the panoramic sweep from Ben Cruachan in the east to the hunched shoulder of Ben Nevis in the north and southward, the Isles of the Sea, Scarba and the Paps of Jura.

There's a Pictish broch on Lismore and a Viking castle, and there's a legend about the island which you would enjoy. It's like the tale of the singing match between Väinämöinen and Joukahainen when they hurl inspired insults at each other in the third rune of the *Kalevala*. Väinämöinen wins the contest and Joukahainen promises him his sister as a prize. In the Lismore story the contest is between two holy men and the prize is the island itself. In AD 562 Moluag and Columba, natives of Ireland, arrived on the west coast of Scotland. They both wanted headquarters for their Christian missions. Each chose Lismore and sought to requisition it by landing there first. Tradition pictures their coracles racing towards the island, oarsmen urged on by the tonsured missionaries. As they approach the shore Moluag sees that his rival's

21

Broch of Tirefuir, Lismore

boat will win. Picking up an axe, he places his little finger on the gunwale, severs it from his hand and throws it on the shingle ahead.

'My flesh and blood have first possession of the island', he cries, 'and I bless it in the name of the Lord'.

Legend makes Columba as bad a loser as Joukahainen. He curses Moluag.

'May you have the alder for your firewood'.

'The Lord will make the alder burn pleasantly', answers Moluag with saintly equanimity.

Columba attacks again.

'May you have the jagged ridges for your pathway'.

'The Lord will smooth them to the feet', replies Moluag, still beyond provocation.

So Moluag got the island.

Columba went north to Iona and became the most famous saint in Celtic history. You had to admit he had a way with words. Imagine replacing the banality of 'Fuck off' with his 'May you have the jagged ridges for your pathway'. I tried it in the school playground. They were all playing at Japs and Americans, running about pretending to be planes, but I couldn't make them out clearly in the fog. I crashed into an American plane when it was aiming to gun down a Jap.

'Out of the way', shouted the American plane.

'May you have the jagged ridges for your pathway', I said.

'Oh fuck off', yelled the plane, 'Ra-ta-ta-ta blam blam!'

'Aieeargh', screamed the Japanese plane, histrionically plummeting in a starfish of arms and legs.

By Loch Lomond, the Pass of Brander and Loch Awe the wartime train ride from Glasgow to Oban

23

Castle Coeffin, Lismore

was sagging luggage racks, cracked leather window straps, roosters of steam, coal smuts and piercing whistles from the guard when it was time to leave each country station along the way. At Oban, chief of north-western Scottish seaboard harbours, the Helsinki of the Highlands, waited the gangway to the 'Lochinvar'. Once aboard there was a visit to the oily, racketing engine room, then up on deck to watch the island of Kerrera slip past on the port side and to starboard, poised over the sea on the brink of its crag, Dunollie Castle, ruined stronghold of the MacDougalls. Lismore was less than an hour away across the Lynn of Lorn, a ribbon of dark green backed by the gaunt hills of Morvern.

In this place of legend, limestone furrows and the stones of Picts and Vikings I gained a father. When he took me to Loch Fiart at the south end of the island to fish for trout from a leaky brown rowing boat the moustache ceased to threaten. Hitler would never have taken me fishing. The island brought me my first glasses, the first stage in the lifting of the fog. When he watched me take the shortest of his split-cane rods and cast a Greenwell's Glory or Silver Butcher into reeds, instead of to the side of them, where the trout lay, my father realized I couldn't see well enough to do important things and the first low-powered spectacles were prescribed.

Our Lismore home was at Kilcheran, a bay-windowed, white-washed boarding house among trees with a view of the sea and a small island called, in Gaelic, *Eilean Na Cloiche* – Island of the Rock – because of its single stack of weathered limestone. The rock was like the Sphinx from one angle, from another, the conning tower of a submarine, so it was a reminder of war even in the peace of that place.

24

25

Kilcheran Islands showing Eilean na Cloiche

26

My father, Harold Walker, (above) ready for a day on the loch, and (right) preparing the rods

There was a big gramophone in the lounge of the boarding house and a pile of abandoned ten-inch records on a sofa, witness to previous boarders' taste in popular music. One record was a puzzle. It was by Flanagan and Allen. I liked the tune but didn't know what to make of the words.

Are you havin' any fun?
What y'gettin' out o' livin'?
What good is what you've got
If you're not havin' any fun?

What *was* fun? My father seemed to have it out on the loch when he went fishing, though he took fishing so seriously, and Roger had what looked like fun, watching for Germans from his gatepost. In the rabbit song the farmer's fun would be a pie if he could shoot the rabbit. Before I sat on him Paul Robeson landed in jail whenever he tried to have fun. Messrs Flanagan and Allen were proposing fun as a pre-condition of success. Whatever it was it didn't seem to me that I was having enough of it to pass the test. No doubt about it, Paul Robeson and I were failures.

Lismore sounds were best at Easter because of the lambs. Their voices blended with the cawing of rooks in the elms, the noises of cattle, the wind and the waves breaking on the shore below the house. Awkwardly, I told my father how much I liked this natural country music and how it made me think of the sounds that came from the gramophone when the white dog on the HMV label spun round. By now I'd got to know heavy, black-labelled twelve-inch records of Liszt's second *Hungarian Rhapsody*, selections from the *Nutcracker Suite* and the Glasgow-born pianist, Frederic Lamond, playing the 'Moonlight' sonata. My father took the cue and brought home more records of classical music, thinking that if his son was to be denied rugby and cricket because of his eyes, he might find occupation through his ears. Beethoven's *Pastoral* was my introduction to the symphony. I loved the second movement especially, 'Scene by the Brook', partly for the imitations of bird song, but mostly for the rhythms of the lower strings which made me think less of a flowing stream than of a small train always carrying me back to Lismore.

***

With the last 'All Clear' and the Japanese surrender 'evacuation' was over. Life slid almost imperceptibly from 'Whitecraigs' back to the city. Everything contained in the idea of home belonged to Lismore so it didn't seem to matter that the city flat had replaced the house on the south side. But now there was serious school, the ignominy of exclusion from games, and getting picked on for being different, a weak-eyed cissy. I need to tell you about the school bully, Sibelius, because I don't think I could have stood up to him without you. Even now he's part of a continuing present, and though I beat him in the end with your help, I still fight him again whenever I'm in what Huckleberry Finn calls 'a close place'.

The bully's name is Douglas. Flanked by his gang of younger toadies he is a minefield I must cross to reach the safety of the top-floor flat. My under-correcting lenses show me no features and the lack of definition gives him a sinister radiance. The head above his thick body is a haloed blob against the light. I fear he may be invincible.

'Where d'you think you're going?' he says, punching my chest.

29

30

Loch Fiart, Lismore, with upgraded boat

I raise my fists without conviction and say, 'Stop that. I'm going home. Please get out of my way'.

'I'm no' in your fuckin' way', he says, slapping the side of my head.

This is the warm-up, I know from the last encounter. He smacks my fist off its hopeless aim and spits. The gang laughs and despair claws up from my stomach to my chest. His next punch knocks my glasses to the gutter. When I bend down to feel for them, two of the gang shove me into the road and spit gobs at my cheek. Douglas punches me in the side. A car swishes past, swerving from the dubious activity spilling from the pavement. I scrabble in the gutter for the glasses, grab them from the muck and put them on.

In staccato breaths I remonstrate with Douglas.

'You're a bully. This isn't fair. You're bigger'n me. Why d'you always pick on me? Why don't you hit someone your own size?'

I have no endowment, no training for this. The war's over, isn't it? Didn't the enemy surrender? These boys live in respectable council houses with gardens or in middle-class red sandstone tenement flats like mine. Why do they act like Nazis or torturing, slitty-eyed Japs? I have done them no harm. Is this Paul Robeson's revenge for the broken record and will it roll on for ever?

'I'm no' bigger'n you', Douglas says.

'Yes you are', I shout, for there must, surely, be a recourse to visible reason, 'Isn't he?' I absurdly appeal to the gang.

'Naw, he's no' bigger'n you', they say, 'he's the same size'.

'Right', says Douglas. He spits on the road, then on his hands. 'Come on an' we'll prove it. Stand back to back wi' me'.

I put my back to his. I will be Moluag to his Columba. He's taller by head and shoulders. The gang sniggers. Douglas reaches his arms backwards to grip my armpits, bends forward to pull me up and over his head. He throws me to the ground. Winded, bleeding from forehead and nose, glasses gone again, I hear the enemy move away.

'Bastard', they call, 'fuckin' bastard, ya fuckin' wee cunt ya, up yur hole ya specky cunt ya'.

The voices fade. Passers-by have shown no interest. When I get home I'll make up something, say I tripped and fell again.

**

It didn't bother me that most school subjects were dull. Daydreams took care of that, though I wondered why so much time had to be wasted. The language classes were thickets of grammar and vocabulary to be penetrated before you might reach an idea to engage the mind. What had Julius Caesar's division of Gaul to do with the way the world looked from a flat above a tram-car terminus at Anniesland Cross? Who could care about Monsieur LeBrun's voyage to his bureau in Paris when the trams went to places called Langside and Elderslie? But the music class made me angry. Even in summer the music room was cold. Sunshine froze when it met the black-and-white glaze of the sol-fa chart that hung over the chalkboard. The black letters of the chart made a headstone for music's grave. Funeral rites were conducted by Miss Stevenson, a wiry, disappointed teacher who mortified herself by wearing blouses too small for her neck and punishing her hair into a crust of ridges. Her head was always over to one side like Robert Louis Stevenson's 'Thrawn Janet'. It wouldn't have been much of a surprise if she'd suddenly caught fire 'an' fell in ashes to the grund'. She had a voice like a duck's.

Dumped once a week into a limbo hour of 'culture' between Maths and Geography, pupils sat in chilled submission. Listless voices dragged behind Miss Stevenson's dry quacks up and down the sol-fa chart or sluggishly intoned 'Men of Harlech' when her bony, imperative fingers stabbed out the accompaniment. The glossy black piano looked like a hearse which had delivered music's corpse for our weekly wake. Nobody misbehaved. Young rebels who would have savaged another teacher for oddity or weakness were demoralized by the woman's brisk, impregnable gloom.

How could this have any connection with the electricities of the *Tannhäuser* Overtures, Beethoven Fifths, the *Polovtsian Dances* and *New World*s I was hearing on the wireless? What could Miss Stevenson's 'Men of Harlech' have to do with the Brahms symphony I heard when my father took me to my first orchestral concert at Glasgow's St Andrew's Hall? For the first time here was a whole symphony orchestra, live, not spinning round on a black shellac disc with Nipper in the middle. This was a choir of instruments getting ready to sing, fanned across a great stage with fragments of imminent music in the players' tuning-up and auspices of splendour in the gold of trumpets, horns and trombones. There was the podium, waiting for the magisterial figure who would call these disparate bodies and instruments to order and harmonize them into collective song. Then the expectant hush after the entry of the leader. The conductor glides across the stage in his tailed black and white, a tall penguin on castors. He mounts the podium, leans to shake hands with the leader, bows to our applause and faces the orchestra. Now the palpable hush when nothing in the world

33

matters except the sounds to come. His baton flicks consciousness into wonder. Arms, lungs and lips, strings and brasses, reeds and the ancient power of stretched skin over copper all moving and voicing together.

Dear Sibelius, the music room changed because of you. Miss Stevenson was replaced by Mr Adams, an elegant, Italianate-looking man with a magic turn of phrase.

'The basic function of the horn in the orchestra', he said, 'is to provide a wad of tone'. Here was real information.

The sol-fa chart was sent to the corner and the Men of Harlech beat their retreat. Mr Adams stood before the class holding a red-label HMV 78 rpm record and told us the story behind *The Swan of Tuonela*.

'The legend is from the *Kalevala*, the Finnish national epic', he said. 'It tells of the land of the dead which is surrounded by a river of black water. The Swan of Tuonela glides majestically down the river, singing. Divided strings and harp represent the river and a solo *cor anglais* the Swan'.

Intoxicated, I ran home to proselytize my parents about the music I had just heard.

'Oh yes', humphed my father, 'Sibelius. He's one of those moderns'. This was ironic, considering your refusal to ape the modernist fashion of Schoenberg and his atonal acolytes.

'Go your own modest but sure way', you tell yourself in a diary note just before your forty-fifth birthday, 'you won't be any the worse for that'. And in a diary-entry in June 1912 you say: 'You won't be any "greater" by outdoing – or trying to outdo – your contemporaries in terms of a revolutionary "profile". Let's not join in any race'.

But I wasn't to be deflated by parental omniscience just as you refused to be intimidated by Schoenberg. With a concert performance of the Second Symphony I was hooked. It hooked my father too. We got into the habit of calling you 'The Big Man'. The more we listened to you the bigger you got.

***

'Forget medicine', the eye specialist said.

He was a dark-suited, square, caustic man with an important title, 'The Queen's Eye Specialist in Scotland'. He had asked me what I wanted to be when I grew up. I wanted to be a doctor.

'That's out of the question', he said. 'You'll be blind by the time you're twenty. Think of something you can do when you can't see. Be a grocer'.

I couldn't follow his reasoning, supposing that, if only for the sake of the customers, blindness would rule out grocery as decisively as it ruled out medicine, but the continuing fog and daily headaches made his prognosis terrifyingly credible. After all his title meant 'Eyes by Appointment' and he wasn't appointing me any at all for the approaching future.

'In the meantime', he said, 'keep your eyes closed as much as possible'.

So, as much as possible, I closed them and kept my ears open. This is how things were when I heard your Second Symphony.

The important-looking envelope on the breakfast table was addressed to me. An aunt who worked at the BBC had organized two tickets for a live-broadcast studio performance by the BBC Scottish Orchestra. Its conductor was Ian Whyte, my one and only boyhood hero. He was one of the most gifted British

35

musicians and would have been more widely known but for the sniffiness of London critics about culture in Scotland, though the BBC in London used to send him new works to be checked for mistakes before they were let loose on other BBC orchestras. His perfect pitch was legendary and his ear always alert. When workmen were busy in the BBC canteen he remarked that one of their chisels had all the basic harmonics of C major. At a rehearsal of Mendelssohn's *Ruy Blas* Overture he turned to his first horn.

'Your note is so pure it has upset the rest of the chord', he said.

Rehearsing a variety programme with Ian Whyte and his orchestra, Sir Harry Lauder realized that the conductor was correcting wrong notes which had crept into his accompaniments through the fault of a careless arranger or copyist.

'But Mr Whyte', exclaimed Sir Harry, 'I've played that music all round the world'.

'Ah weel, Sir Harry', replied Mr Whyte, 'ye've been playing it wrang'.

The first musical sounds Ian Whyte heard were the ding and clang of hammer and anvil in his grandfather's smithy and the folk music the old man played on his fiddle at home in the evening. He learned to read music faster than words and had memorized Handel's *Messiah* when he was six. At ten he crossed the River Forth from his native Dunfermline to play the organ at Dalmeny Kirk, furious that his feet wouldn't reach the pedals. At the Royal College of Music he was taught by Stanford and Vaughan Williams, then returned to Scotland to extemporize piano backgrounds for silent films. After a spell as resident musician to Baron Glentanar of Aboyne and another as the first Director of Music for the BBC in Scotland, he became principal conductor of the orchestra that was about to play your Second Symphony. Tonight, with me in the invited audience. My father had come too, to see what Sibelius, this modern, could do.

Sibelius, you knew about Ian Whyte before I did. His son, a journalist with perfect recall, told me what happened.

'Father came home from the BBC in high spirits holding a piece of paper', he said. 'It was a telegram from Sibelius. It took days to get through wartime security checks. Sibelius had heard Father's broadcast performance of the Second Symphony from Glasgow on his wireless up in Finland. He wanted to thank Father for playing his symphony properly. Father was over the moon'.

'Thank you, Ian Whyte and orchestra, for playing my Second Symphony as I intended it to be heard – Jean Sibelius'.

The two of you never met outside your music, but Ian Whyte did visit Scandinavia when King Haakon invited him to conduct the National Radio Orchestra in Oslo.

'All my life I have wanted to be a conductor', said the King.

'How kind, sir', Whyte replied. 'All my life I have wanted to be a king'.

The red light comes on. Now we are live, on air. The lady announcer introduces the concert to listeners sitting by their radios. Ian Whyte walks across the studio floor to his orchestra. He crouches like a tense, dark monkey, baton outstretched. His conjuring, urgent stick jabs the air. He's not graceful to watch and there's nothing in him of the showman.

38

Sibelius's residence in Rapallo

He's a diviner, his baton a wand that finds the notes in the air, or a casting fisherman, catching the notes and miraculously joining them together a split second before they reach the ear.

Sibelius, the opening bars of your Second Symphony are like an accompaniment looking for a partner until the arrival of the dancing woodwind theme which meets the need and carries the music forward. After a series of youthful string quartets, works composed before your Third Symphony seemed to proclaim you a patriotic composer whose special gifts for musical narrative and the evocation of Finnish landscape were dedicated to the creation of a vigorous new myth of the Finnish nation. Nationalism was thought to inform the Tchaikovskian finale of the First Symphony and even the blazing conclusion of the Second. We now know that you weren't thinking in particular about your country's yearning for nationhood, though maybe your sense of yourself as a Finn always kept Finnish aspirations alive at an unconscious level. Don Juan and the Stone Guest were on your mind and you were keenly affected by the light and landscapes of the Italian Riviera when you began to sketch the Second Symphony during a stay at Rapallo in 1901. In the wake of Keats, Shelley, Henry James, Goethe, Wagner, Renoir and Monet you'd gone to Italy knowing, like Miss Lavish in E. M. Forster's *Room with a View,* that 'one doesn't come to Italy for niceness…one comes for life'. There's a plaque on the building you stayed in:

FUGGENDO LE NORDICHE BRUME
DAL FEBBRAIO AL MAGGIO 1901
QUI SOGGIORNO
JEAN SIBELIUS
DI TIRRENICA LUCE INTRISA L'ALATA FANTASIA
IVI COMPOSE LA SUA
2A SINFONIA OP. 43
NEL 1O CENTENARIO DELLA NASCITA
1865 – 1965

———————

LA CITTA DI RAPALLO
E
IL CIRCOLO ARTISTICO CULTURALE
DEL TIGULLIO[1]

[1] ESCAPING THE NORDIC MISTS
FROM FEBRUARY TO MAY 1901
HERE RESIDED JEAN SIBELIUS
THE TIRRENIAN LIGHT GAVE FLIGHT TO HIS
IMAGINATION
HERE HE COMPOSED HIS 2ND SYMPHONY OP. 43
[This plaque was erected]
ON THE FIRST ANNIVERSARY OF HIS BIRTH
1865 – 1965
[By]
THE CITY OF RAPALLO
AND
THE ART AND CULTURAL SOCIETY OF TIGULLIO

In a hotel across the piazza Nietzsche began work on *Also Sprach Zarathustra* in 1882 and the Garden of Ezra Pound is a few steps away.

You wandered to nearby Chiavari.

'The sea is raging violently', you wrote to the conductor, Robert Kajanus, 'The waves seem as big as houses … it is moonlight and the clouds wander heavy with woe'.

The Stone Guest, turbulent Mediterranean and woeful clouds help us to understand the brass eruptions in the second movement of the Symphony, declamations hostile to human striving. The modulation to pianissimo strings brings momentary ease of spirit. After the first trumpeted statement of the heroic tune from which the finale grows, billowing strings carry you into cathedral spaces. You stumble and lose direction, but, like Parsifal, you find your way back.

The apotheosis has come and gone, followed by the silence which always asks, 'How does life go on when the music stops?' The truth of this music had nothing to do with a God who inflicts pain to prove his power by curing it, nothing to do with the triviality of playing or not playing games at school or with the fog. A voice had spoken mysteriously but with uncanny intimacy in a code beyond any capacity of words. This was, somehow, the utterance I would have made if I'd known how to make it.

'Yes, that's right, that's right', I wanted to shout, 'That's what I mean too. That's what it's like'.

Paul Robeson had sympathized, but now I was completely understood. Later I discovered that Mendelssohn, echoing Schopenhauer, had perfectly defined the power of musical language: 'It's not that music is too vague for words; it's too precise for words'.

41

42

'Waves ... as big as houses' - Chiavari

In notes for a recording of the Symphony in 1954 Leopold Stokowski, said: 'Each time I go to Finland to conduct I am struck by the immense strength and vitality of Sibelius as a man, also by his infinite range of thought, feeling and imagination, and by his closeness to Nature... Just as Rembrandt, El Greco and many other painters have made portraits of themselves in colour, so has Sibelius, perhaps unconsciously, made a portrait of himself in tone, in his Second Symphony. His music is like a song of all the people, and all the forests and lakes of his country. Although in classical form, it is a free and rhapsodic expression of Sibelius's inner life of feeling and fantastic imagination − it is the essence of Finland. The grandiloquence of the Symphony's finale has often been interpreted as a raised, Finnish freedom-fist; but perhaps it more universally expresses an affirmation of life over death as well as Sibelius's own sense of his potential future as a composer of the questing soul'.

On the walk home my father stopped by a street lamp, turned to me.

'Grand', he said, 'grand'. Long pause. 'He's a big man. Grand', he said, and held out his hand for me to shake.

***

Soon afterwards Douglas the bully and his gang closed with me for the last time. I was walking home from school, thinking of Lismore. It would be Easter soon and I'd be back with the lambs, the limestone crags, the rooks in the Kilcheran elms, the sea. I had been given a shiny new black 'sou' wester'. Its size was 'Small Gent's'. I would fish with my father in oilskinned companionship. My fly-casting would be

43

more accurate, I hoped, because the Queen's Eye Specialist in Scotland had prescribed stronger lenses so that I could catch and store as much as possible of the world before the blindness came. I'd keep my line clear of the reeds. I had even been allowed to go to the pictures at the local cinema. There, craning my neck up from the front row, I gorged my imagination on the mysteries and gangster movies of film noir, building a black-and-white fantasy life of portentous dialogue and shadow-laden camera work, shady characters and twisted love. I made up my own anthology of hard-boiled, romantic speeches.

I was a psychotic Robert Ryan in *Caught* giving the word to Barbara Bel Geddes.

'You know enough about me to know that I can't stand losing', I tell her, 'Only nice people lose'. There's tough.

I was Humphrey Bogart in *The Maltese Falcon*, outwitting the fat man, taking what he wants from Mary Astor but sending her over for murdering his partner. 'Now you're really dangerous', he says to Astor. What a line to have ready for the right girl.

One day, when the acne dried up, I'd be the two-timing Jack Palance in *Sudden Fear*.

'I'm so crazy about you I could break your bones', he tells his mistress, Gloria Grahame.

Walking away from the girl who sold me *Finlandia*, I'd toss that to her over my world-weary shoulder. She'd run after me, give me back my money and we'd go off and listen to the record together.

I was Clifton Webb using wit to outclass his wife's lover in *The Dark Corner*.

'I probably shan't return before dawn', he says. 'How I detest the dawn. The grass looks like it's been left out all night'.

Most of all I was Bogart in *Dark Passage*. Lauren

44

Bacall would look at me, eyes a little hooded, mouth a little pouty.

'When I get excited about something, I give it everything I've got', she'd tell me huskily. 'I'm funny that way'.

In return for everything she'd got I'd take her to Lismore. We'd walk by the sea and climb the Bàrr Mòr. We'd be silhouetted against skies of giant clouds and orange sunsets, understanding each other without need of words. We'd listen to *The Swan of Tuonela* on the gramophone. But there were shady characters to deal with first.

There is no parleying this time. Douglas is planted in front of me, the gang at my back.

'Hiya, Specky', he says with the first quick punch.

Laughter behind me and one goading voice, 'Belt him tae fuck, Dougie, on ye go'.

I shake my head and see the beatific island invaded, the great garden contaminated by filthy language and brute power. Nazi feet march and the death camps' living skeletons appeal without hope from the newsreels of their liberation. Rage and revulsion cauterize fear of the enemy. My fists snap into position, up and out. Douglas's punch hasn't knocked off my glasses and with the new lenses I can see him well enough that my first return punch catches his ear. Incredulous, he flinches, steps back. A trumpet calls the fanfare theme from the last movement of your Second Symphony. I side-step his next punch, feint with my left and with my right send pure war into his mouth. Not a sound from the gang. Douglas drops his guard and staggers, spitting blood. He tries to speak, holds up his hands, palms outward, as if to push me away.

'Wait. Wait a minute. You're no' fightin' the right way'. He sags forward, coughs blood at the pavement.

I skip back, then run at him to pummel his face and belly.

I move back again, dancing now, and a voice behind me shouts, 'Aw, for fuck's sake, Dougie, melt the cunt, whit's wrang wi ye?'

The Symphony builds its cathedral song of strings and my fists ring with the pulsing brass and woodwind. Douglas is down and I'm on him, legs scissored round his waist, squeezing the breath from him, while I grip his hair. I will smash his head on the pavement until he's dead.

Another voice, 'Specky, Specky, for fuck's sake stop it, you're gonny fuckin' kill him'.

Douglas is moaning. I hear running feet, the gang deserting. The symphony ends. I smack Douglas in the face twice with my open hand, roll off him and walk away.

The music begins again. Not the Second Symphony now, but the three-note motive of 'Lemminkäinen's Homeward Journey', the fourth of your *Legends from the Kalevala*. My childhood, whatever it was, is over. I am the lover and adventurer of the thirtieth rune of the *Kalevala*, and you, Sibelius, are Tiera, my trusty ally with your spear of perfect balance. We have vanquished Pakko Pakkanen, the freezer of Pohjola, squeezing the bitter weather from him. My shady characters have been transubstantiated into the galloping rondo of a hero's homecoming:

Then the wayward Lemminkäinen
Turned his troubles into horses
And his cares to great black geldings;
All his bad times into bridles,

And the secret hates to saddles.
Leaped upon the horse's back.
On the white-blaze horse's back,
Rode away with comrade Tiera,
Homeward to his gentle mother,
To his much-respected parent.

When I get home this time I'll tell them what really happened. I beat the master race. I saved the island. But not single-handed, Sibelius. Me and the Big Man.

2. Valse Triste

The dark brown wireless sat high on the sitting room mantelpiece, ruling the room. In war or peace it told the only truth. BBC was the ubiquitous, infallible voice. British six o'clock news, British cricket, British Churchill, British *Dick Barton, Special Agent*.

Dear Sibelius, one afternoon the voice was wordless and foreign. Yours. The announcer called it 'Symphony Number 3 in C'.

When the second movement came my arms reached up to catch and hold the tune.

Quickly, then, downstairs from the top-floor flat to the street to 'play' but really to be alone with the music. I'd need to keep my eye on the time. I had no watch, but at 7.30 pm they'd hang a flag from my bedroom window which would mean time for home and bed. Today 'playing' meant sitting on a wall despoiled of its iron railings for the recent industries of war and hugging your new, ineffable tune.

The signal flapped at the window, a rusty Union Jack from wartime patriotisms. I must be prompt to avoid reprimand. I began to climb the stairs and checked my mind. The tune had gone. Panic gripped my chest, flushed sweat into my face. My arms were dead. I couldn't go home like this, leaving the tune behind.

I looked back into the street. A man and woman were walking along the pavement, pleasantly arm in arm.

'They'll know', I thought.

I ducked back down to the street, stumbled up to them. They stopped, non-plussed, beginning to be wary.

'Excuse me', I managed to say, 'can you help me?

I've lost, I mean I can't remember a magic thing that happened...'

They smiled implausibly, drew closer together, swerved past me and quickened their steps. I went back into the maw of the tenement.

In bed I pulled the darkness round me and tried to think of a strategy. With hoarded pocket money I had bought for 3/6d a Pelican Book called *The Symphony*. Bringing my bedside lamp under the quilt to muffle the brightness so they wouldn't know I was awake from tell-tale light under the bedroom door, I switched it on and took the book from the bedside table. The chapter about you had commentaries on all seven of your symphonies. When I looked up the second movement of Number 3 in C major it referred to Ex. 19 at the end of the chapter in a way that I knew it was the magic theme. I fingered the stave, willing the hieroglyphs to enter my skin, tried to hum the first notes but they didn't sound in key and I couldn't read anything from page to sound beyond the fifth note though the quotation went on for another bar. Then I decided what to do and set the alarm clock for 6.30 am.

When she saw me so early in the kitchen my mother thought apocalypse. I nearly gagged on the toast and tea, but got them down, muttered something about comparing homework with a classmate before the start of school and ran down the stairs with *The Symphony* in my blazer pocket.

The school was down Woodend Drive. This morning it would never end; but at 8.20 by the school clock, breathless from the run, I reached the door of the Music Room and lay in wait. Mr Adams arrived at

50

Mr Eric Adams

8.30 to collect whatever he needed before going down to the big hall to play the piano for Prayers.

'Good morning', he said, surprised to find a lone pupil waiting for him so early in the day, 'Why...?'

'Excuse me, Mr Adams, please could you play this for me before Prayers, it's very short, but please play it because I can't remember it properly, it's very important and I really don't feel very well just now if you know what I mean because it's gone away...'

Mr Adams held out his hand for the book, glanced at Ex. 19. There was no condescension in his smile.

'Let's go to the piano', he said.

He sat on the piano stool, put the book on the music stand and brought his long hands down to the keys. Your spell was in the air again. It was in my brain and skin and my arms were warm and strong.

We went down to Prayers.

'Thank you very much, Mr Adams, I...'

He said, 'I know what you mean'.

***

There you are in London, Sibelius, briskly exiting from Victoria railway station. It's February 1908. Cold for England, but no problem for a Finn. You've come to conduct the Third Symphony at the invitation of the composer, Sir Granville Bantock, on behalf of the Royal Philharmonic Society. You're full of anticipation and feel greatly honoured.

'It will be strange', you think, 'to stand on the same podium where everyone from Haydn to Tchaikovsky has conducted his own music'.

You recall your talk with Mahler when he visited Helsinki a few months ago. When you discussed the symphony you said you 'admired its style and severity of form and the profound logic that created an inner connection between all the motives'. Mahler's opinion was just the opposite.

'No!' he said, 'The symphony must be like the world. It must be all-embracing'.

Mahler had just completed his Faustian Eighth Symphony, the colossal 'Symphony of a Thousand'. You had just finished composing your Third.

This would appear to set you and Mahler in opposition, Mahler as the latter-day, warm-blooded Romantic. As Neville Cardus puts it: 'Mahler not only wore his heart on his sleeve; he exposed lungs and liver'. By contrast, you might seem to be a buttoned-up formalist, coolly organizing sounds in logical patterns. Wrong, of course. Just because you don't vivisect yourself in public doesn't mean you lack vital organs, and if your music displays reverence for form it's also full of energy.

The Symphony is a new departure, compact, genial and athletic. It supersedes the opulences of your first two and is the least self-questioning of your seven. In Finland it's been hailed as 'music in its newest and most sublime form…revolutionary, and truly Sibelian'. But you're anxious, understandably. The Second Symphony was a hard act to follow, not only because of its spectacular success in Finland. When you conducted it in Berlin three years ago you became, overnight, one of the most controversial names in German musical life. One critic said you were more inventive than Richard Strauss; but could you sustain the achievement? Had you laid a foundation for growth? They didn't much like the Third in Russia, but you had one distinguished critic. Young Sergei Prokofiev was in the audience when you conducted it in St Petersburg. He wrote a passage for solo cello in an orchestration exercise for his teacher, Rimsky-Korsakov, who was not amused.

53

'What's this?' asked Rimsky. 'Why have you only one cello playing the melody?'

'Because I don't like it when all the cellos play together', said Prokofiev.

'You don't? Have you ever heard them?'

'Yesterday', replied Prokofiev, 'in Sibelius's symphony'.

'God in heaven', barked Rimsky, 'Sibelius! Why listen to Sibelius?'

'The new symphony has none of the character of this previously much respected and admired composer', wrote the music critic for the *St Petersburg Herald*, 'Is it really possible that he has already written himself out?'

Galling, but just as usual: the people who write about the thing always think they know better than the people who make the thing. You're sure that with this scrupulously concentrated music you have written yourself definitively in, achieving the formal pliancy and patrician voice you'll need for future symphonies.

'Never pay any attention to what critics say', you told a friend, 'Remember, a statue has never been set up in honour of a critic'.

As you mingle with Londoners you wonder how a British audience will respond to the throaty mutter of cellos and basses – eight of each – at the beginning of the Symphony and the way you turn up the volume to make the music stride so quickly across space towards the listener. You know you've got an exquisite trick up your sleeve in the gently rocking melody of the slow movement before what you call the 'crystallization of ideas from chaos' in the finale. From a kaleidoscope of thematic hints you draw a stately hymn-like tune into the foreground

54

to carry the music into the C-major security of what Sir Donald Tovey calls the Symphony's 'one and all-sufficing climax'. It's energy, packed, lithe and radiant.

With classical economy you filter out the prolixities of late Romanticism to make an essentially Romantic claim about the shaping power of imagination. While you head for the City you're unavoidably rehearsing. The music plays from your mind to the winter air of England, bringing these bustling foreign streets into the kingdom of your big tune.

Bantock, your best friend in Britain, and dedicatee of the Third Symphony, wasn't at the station to meet you as arranged because you've taken an earlier train than planned. Eventually he runs you to earth sitting comfortably in a tea-shop at Oxford Circus. Musicians start to play. You lay your hand on Bantock's arm.

'They are playing my *Valse Triste*', you say, 'Isn't it strange that it should be the first music I hear on this visit to England?'

So you see, Sibelius, *Valse Triste* and the Third Symphony intersected for you then in London as they would for me fifty years later in Scotland.

***

'It's lovely, wise music', my mother said.

I knew my father was still too enthralled by his recent discovery of the Second Symphony to be ready, quite yet, for something new. His favourite hum while shaving was the theme which propels the finale to the trumpet-tongued citadel of its ending. So he was beginning every day on a high with The Big Man. How grateful we were to you, Sibelius, for evicting the Mikado, Jack Point and the Pirates of Penzance from our master's morning voice. Last night we'd all listened to Brahms, but tonight he'd probably say, 'Let's have the Second'. No need to mention your name: there was only one 'Second'. This would mean that after the dinner things were put away and the dishes washed we'd make a semi-circle round the record player – persistently, for us, still a 'gramophone' – and listen together in the tiny sitting-room as if we were in a great yet exclusive concert hall with Eugene Ormandy and the Philadelphia Orchestra. His initiation into the magic of Ex. 19 would have to wait. So my missionary fervour fastened on my less conservative mother. She listened in silence to the newly acquired LP of Symphony Number 3 until I lifted the pick-up at the end of the second movement.

'A friend of Sibelius's thought the tune was like a child's prayer', I said.

'Yes, it's lovely', she said again. 'It begins on tiptoe, like a child going into a room full of grown-ups'.

'If it's a prayer, why does he break up the tune and seem to question it?'

'He's testing its strength, maybe to see if it can hold its own with the grown-ups. It's wistful, dreamlike and appealing, but there's acceptance as well. That's a kind of strength'.

'Will the prayer get an answer?'

'It deserves to. It reminds me of *Valse Triste*. That's my favourite. I think it'll always be my favourite'.

'Why?'

'Because of my father – your grandfather', she said, 'and because of my soldier brother, your uncle Marshall'.

So it happened that the spell of Ex. 19 raised two Sibelian spirits, father and son. And this is why I'm

56

Nora K. Mitchell, my 'less conservative mother'

asking you, Sibelius, to time-travel with me into a sense of two lives which pay you tribute because, though I didn't know it until my mother spoke as she did that day about *Valse Triste*, they both loved your music long before I did.

First we'll meet Grandfather out for a Sunday stroll in Glasgow. We'll follow him to a railway junction near the snow-bound city of Arbroath in the north-east of Scotland in December 1906; then we'll go to find his son, my mother's soldier, the uncle I never met, in northern Greece and Macedonia, briefly visible before passing 'out of the sight of men' on the World War I battleground of the Salonika Front in 1917.

***

On a hot Sunday afternoon in June 1906 John Marshall Mitchell, wheat merchant, walks in the Glasgow park, his wife, Isa, on his arm. They're a handsome couple, formally dressed because they've just come from morning church. He's a very tall man in his early fifties.

'Your father's six feet, pressed down and running over', Isa would tell her children.

She is ten years younger and almost a foot shorter. John is solid, philosophically inclined and once laid a wreath on the grave of Thomas Carlyle. She basks in his security, but is disposed to be impish and is the one person who knows how to make her husband unbend.

On Friday evenings the Mitchell family sings. The upright piano, never quite in tune, is angled across a corner of the living room at 211 West Princes Street, Glasgow, left of the high bay window. The three daughters, Nora my mother and her sisters, Mary

58

and Jessie, line up in the bay with twelve year-old big brother Marshall behind them to give a semblance of bass under the girls' quivery treble. John stands in pride of place, in front of the piano where he can keep an eye on his children and enjoy the sway of Isa's competent little body on the music stool as her hands ripple across the keyboard, loud pedal firmly down. There's no sheet music on the stand: Isa has her repertoire by heart and even Nora, the youngest daughter, soon knows that proceedings will begin with 'Jock o' Hazeldean' and conclude fortissimo with 'Up with the Bonnets o' Bonnie Dundee'. Between the familiar Scottish songs there'll be Isa's favourite snippets of Bach, Chopin and Mendelssohn. John's business requires him to travel and he sometimes has to be away from home on Friday. If so, he can be sure that the following week's concert will include eighteenth-century Jean Adam's 'There's nae luck aboot the hoose' about the husband who comes home bringing good luck with him. Isa will sing the first verse solo, then lead the children into the chorus, glancing up archly across the piano at her contentedly blushing husband.

And are ye sure the news is true?
And are ye sure he's weel?
Is this a time to think o' wark?
Ye jauds, fling by your wheel.
Is this a time to think o'wark,
When Colin's at the door?
Rax me my cloak, I'll to the quay,
And see him come ashore.
For there's nae luck aboot the hoose,
There's nae luck at a',
There's little pleasure in the hoose
When oor gudeman's awa'.

60

John and Isa Mitchell

When the sun shines in Scotland you make the most of it. Scotland's a bit like Finland that way. On this cloudless Sunday afternoon the broad lawns of the park, sloping down to the River Kelvin, have almost disappeared under a patchwork of people. There are picnics, rolled-up shirt sleeves, Italian ice-creams, children with skipping ropes and bats and balls, cuddling sweethearts, improvised newspaper hats to protect pale Scottish skins.

'John, dear, will you not take off your jacket, for you must be boiling?' says Isa, who has removed the crocheted black shawl she uses when she goes to the draughty Presbyterian church which always keeps its cool.

'No thank you, my dear', answers John, patting the watch in his waistcoat pocket, 'It's still the Sabbath. All day'.

They walk towards the rotunda where a brass band is pulverizing *The Nutcracker Suite* with a surplus of tuba and trombone.

'Doesn't the Sugar Plum Fairy sound grumpy!' says Isa.

They find a postage-stamp of grass among the picnickers. John's Calvinist rectitude yields to chivalry. He takes off his jacket and spreads it on the ground for his wife to sit on – then, a little stiffly, joins her.

After gale-force selections from *Carmen* the bandmaster turns to address his inattentive audience of sun-worshippers.

'We conclude our concert with an arrangement of a new piece. It's what you might call an atmospheric waltz by the modern Finnish composer, Jean Sibelius. The title is "Valse Triste" and we hope you'll enjoy it. Thank you, Ladies and Gentlemen, and a very good afternoon to you all on this glorious day'.

Isa Mitchell and her children

You can tell right away that the musicians have been saving their best efforts for this daring, modern finale. Feats of unbrazen delicacy are performed on the gleaming, inappropriate instruments and the main theme enters, just as it should, like a sigh. John feels Isa's response to the rhythm of the waltz and slips his arm round her as she tucks her small shoulder into his. They move discreetly together as the music whirls to its peak before the whispered farewell.

'Oh, John, how strange and beautiful', says Isa as he helps her up from his rumpled jacket and gives it a shake in which you might detect Presbyterian admonition for his Sabbath lapse into worldly enjoyment. 'What name did he say for the composer?'

'It sounded like an old Latin name, but he said the composer comes from Finland'.

A few days later John brings Isa the sheet music for *Valse Triste* in a piano reduction. She practises for a month, then includes it in the family's Friday programmes. It becomes a hit with everyone, but especially with John.

***

Now it's the following December. We see John among travellers in the railway station at Arbroath, stranded by snow since early morning. They clap chilled hands and stamp numbed feet on the platform. Their breath sketches brief plumes of body air on the frigid haze. Business has condemned John to the snow-bound north-east, far from home, between Christmas and New Year. Today is Friday the 28th. He's in a bad humour not only because he's bitterly cold, like everyone else, but because he'll miss his cherished evening at the piano with Isa and the children.

Roads are blocked by snow drifts up to twenty feet deep, telephones and telegraphs are out of action and rail traffic is at a standstill because of a derailment between Arbroath and Dundee. John's next appointment is in Dundee. After that he'll go home.

Shortly after 3 pm, the Caledonian Railway Company's local train is ready to depart for Dundee. Its four leading coaches are off the platform, so fifty passengers scramble into the five carriages in the rear. John climbs thankfully into the last carriage. The train chugs tentatively into the falling snow, then comes unexpectedly to a stop at Elliot Junction to allow a northbound train to pass. There is desultory conversation in the last carriage, enough to fog the windows, blanking out the gunmetal North Sea on one side of the track and the white-out of roads and buildings on the other side. John thinks at home it'll soon be time for 'Jock o' Hazeldean' and *Valse Triste*. He remembers his summer happiness in the park.

Back in Arbroath, with the breakdown of normal signalling procedures, it's been decided to substitute a primitive time-interval system to regulate the movement of the trains. Fifteen minutes behind the local for Dundee the long-delayed North British Railway special has been demoted from 'express' status because of the weather and left on its return journey to Edinburgh in blinding snow. It's running tender first because Arbroath has no turntable big enough to accommodate one of the company's biggest engines. The line should be clear by now but twice the driver is stopped and cautioned about what may lie ahead on the track. He has taken 'something to keep the cold out' before steaming out of Arbroath station and picking up speed.

Sibelius, no composer has achieved so consummate a mind of winter as you do in *Tapiola* your last and greatest symphonic poem. The music is starkly monothematic, an extreme concentration on a single idea, monotonally keyed to B minor until a final, easing resolution into B major. At the request of your publisher you provided four lines of verse as the 'programme' of the work:

> Wide-spread they stand, the Northland's
> dusky forests,
> Ancient, mysterious, brooding savage dreams;
> Within them dwells the Forest's mighty God
> And wood-sprites in the gloom weave magic
> secrets.

But this is too picturesque; it domesticates the 'magic secrets', diminishing the chill and the apprehension of colossal emptiness. Your wood-sprites are no kin to a mini-anthropoid Puck or go-between Ariel; they're spears of wind and shards of light glittering from icicles, reflected by snow-caked branches along interminable corridors of quintessential cold. The music's an apotheosis of unpeopled nature. The sub-zero dynamism of Finnish Northland may terrify us – we may try to personify it down to the scale of human malignity by using words like 'hostile', 'savage' or 'brutal' – but you understand that it's purely and impersonally itself, as far from considerations of human reason or divine protection as the iceberg that sank the *Titanic*, the tsunami that devastated Aceh, the earthquake that killed 50,000 in Pakistan a few months later or the snow that fell on Arbroath and the Elliot railway junction in December 1906.

The shock and thunder of collision are simul-taneous. Monstrously exploding through the snow, the North British locomotive crashes into the stationary local at an estimated speed of thirty miles an hour.

67

The overturned locomotive, North British Railway 324
Photograph by permission of Angus Council Cultural Services

68

Rear carriage of the Caledonian Railway local train after the crash
Photograph by permission of Angus Council Cultural Services

The last three carriages of the local are impacted into a carcass of splintered timbers and twisted metal. The North British engine mounts the wreckage and turns over, its drive wheels still revolving.

The moaning of the injured begins. Survivors from both trains start to remove the dead and wounded from the debris. Medical help arrives from Arbroath in two special engines. With the other twenty dead John Mitchell is laid out for identification in the waiting-room of the junction's little station, covered with a white sheet.

At 6.30 pm in the living room of 211 West Princes Street Isa twirls the music stool to the height she likes and smiles at her children. News of the catastrophe doesn't reach them until the grimly formal messenger from the railway company rings the door-bell next morning. This will be the last of the Friday evenings, but not the end of music in the Mitchell household. Now and for the rest of her life, at any time of day, Isa may abruptly abandon kitchen, laundry or conversation. She'll go to the piano. There, we may suppose, she finds relief, an outlet for controlled emotion and the solace of memory in playing and singing from the familiar repertoire. The children grow accustomed to these impromptu recitals. Sometimes one of them will ask:

'Mother, please, *Valse Triste* – for father?'

***

Nora's soldier's name, like his father's, is John Marshall Mitchell. In a fashion of the time he's known to family and friends by his second name. He's promoted to full Lieutenant on 14 November 1916. He's 22 and serving on the Salonika Front with the 11th Battalion, The Cameronians (Scottish Rifles). Compared to the Western Front, Gallipoli and other theatres of war, the Salonika Front was often considered a sideshow. The Allied army was known back home as the 'Gardeners of Salonika' due to the apparent lack of action.

'If you want a holiday, go to Salonika', people would say.

Before Salonika he has enlisted jauntily enough, like thousands of patriotic young men; he has received a short course in musketry and embarked for active service in France. There he bivouacs in fields and has his first taste of chaotic trenches, shelling, comrades killed by grenades and sniper-fire, and gas.

In November 1915 the Battalion sails for Salonika on two ships, one ironically called the *RMS Arcadian*, the other, which carries 2/Lt Mitchell, more appropriately named *HMS Terrible*. After taking on coal at Alexandria the Battalion leaves for Salonika. They are escorted by *HMS Majestic*. The scriptwriter is having sport with the names of the shipping

Weather is bad at Salonika. The movement from quay to camp is a story of rain, wind, tents in snow, digging drains and latrines. The ground freezes and is then heated to slush by a hot sun. Soldiers work on the firing line, establishing gun emplacements. Patrick Downey, a shell-shocked nineteen year-old Private of the 6th Battalion Leinster Regiment, refuses to wear his cap and obey the order to fall in. His division has been mauled at Gallipoli before being transferred to Salonika where the men have been forced to retreat in the face of Bulgarian attack, then dumped for two days in a tented camp in freezing mud. Downey is court-martialled and sentenced to death. When he hears the sentence he laughs.

'That's a good joke', he says, 'you let me enlist and then bring me out here and shoot me'.

70

2nd Lieutenant John Marshall Mitchell

J. Marshall Mitchell
2nd Lieut
11th Cameronians
March
1915

The Officer Commanding British Forces in Greece doesn't see the joke.

'The condition of discipline in the Battalion is such as to render an exemplary punishment highly desirable'.

A few days before Christmas Patrick Downey is executed by firing squad.

Sibelius, looking out at the world from your beloved Finland, you watch the gangsters of Europe murdering their young. Is civilization coming to an end? You brood on the twists and darknesses of the human mind.

'I fear that all the bitter conflicts that are in the air will not resolve themselves only in war', you say, 'Humanity's hatred and wrath have frightening depths'.

From the windows of 'Ainola' you see Russian troops on the highway. 'Our cross', you call them, winding history back to what your people call 'The Great Hostility', when Swedish power over Finland came to an end. It's 1710. The soldiers of the Tsar violate the Karelia, invading the province of Viipuri. The ancient castle is besieged and taken. 'The dwellings are burned to the ground, the people killed in the war. Mother Finland sits in the snowdrifts with her shivering children'. All wars are the same for mothers and children.

On a personal level this war brings intensified financial distress. Regulations against products from enemy countries mean that your German publisher, Breitkopf und Härtel, can't send you royalties.

'My family needs money; think of the children!' you exclaim in your diary, 'My German publisher cannot send anything because of the war. How shall I manage?'

Luckily the London offices of Breitkopf und Härtel are administered by neutral Swiss. Your symphonies are out of bounds but *Finlandia* and *Valse Triste,* your 'greatest hits', can still be played in the wartime repertory of the Allies.

Lieutenant Mitchell is not especially musical; but Friday evenings at home before Elliot Junction and Isa's impromptu recitals have installed in him a small anthology of tunes which help to sustain him in the trenches of the Salonika Front. Sibelius, your famous waltz travelled to a tragic battlefield a long way from both Finland and Scotland. No royalty was paid either to you or to the soldier who took it with him to Greece; but there was something extraordinary, something, perhaps, miraculous.

***

The Cameronians' War Diary for 1916 mainly reports 'situation normal', which seems to mean 'nil gains and nil casualties'. In May the twelve-pounder on *HMS Agamemnon* brings down a Zeppelin said to have been a present from the Kaiser to Ferdinand of Bulgaria. There are practice advances, parades and polishings. Cold, wet weather yields to spring warmth in April 1917. A field ambulance doctor is sniped through the jaw while tending the wounded. A Transport Officer shoots himself to kill his consciousness of the madness. Mills grenades explode in the pockets of two corpses, mutilating the feet of the soldiers who tramped on them. Men go down with malaria.

Early May is dry and warm. The War Lords telegraph each other injunctions, posturings, cross-purposes, accommodations. A Private shoots himself in the foot while cleaning his rife. On 4th May Lieutenant Marshall Mitchell posts his last letter home. It arrives at 211 West Princes Street postmarked 8 May 1917, a few hours before he passes 'out of the sight of men'. Stamped over the handwritten address is a triangle enclosing the crown symbol and the message, 'Passed by Censor: No. 2223'. Presumably this indicates that Marshall's was letter number 2223 from this field post office, not that the Allies had installed 2223 censors to compound other lunacies of the Salonika Front.

It's the letter of a devoted son and brother. He has been man of the house for over ten years, since his father's death in the snow at Elliot Junction. He urges Isa to take care of herself and not to overwork, his two older sisters to help her and Nora to keep on with her swimming at the baths for the good of her health. The rest of the letter expresses acceptance of his circumstances and his faith in a caring, almighty God:

> We are still out of the trenches having a quiet rest, and are appreciating it immensely. The sun is frightfully hot during the day, but at night it is fine and cool. We are wearing sun helmets of course and need them too for the heat is no joke at present.
>
> I am keeping very fit and well, owing to our present conditions which comprise plenty of food and sleep, and my mind is at complete rest in the knowledge that there's still 'luck aboot the hoose' and things are going on happily and well in my home. You have no idea, dear mother-of-mine, how that fact cheers up a man under conditions similar to those in which I am at present placed.
>
> In your letters, dearest, you have always appeared joyful and you have always manifested a great faith that having one common meeting-

74

place, all would be well…I pray to God that this faith may accompany you always and that it may be mine more and more. Be joyful and place your burdens on the shoulder of the Lord, and he will sustain thee, as he does all who come to him. He has carried me through unhurt hitherto, and if it be his will he will continue to do so.

Thus you see it is not 'Valse Triste', but is out of our human hands altogether.

On 7th May the Battalion's human hands prepare equipment for moving into the line. Positions are taken up in trenches on the west side of Lake Doiran. The next day the enemy is bombarded, Bulgarian batteries reply and the southern end of the lake is lit by cascades of fire and flame. The effect is as if lightning were striking each knoll repeatedly in a freak storm. A mist drifts in from the lake, mingles with the smoke of explosives and lies over the gullies in a reeking cloud. At 21.45 two companies of the Scottish Rifles move forward. They are soon lost in the fog and out of radio contact. Lieutenant Mitchell is in No. 2 Company. Senior officers peer into the murk. At first they can be optimistic: in the glare of searchlights soldiers appear to be scrambling into enemy trenches. Then the mist takes over and there is only the thump of the big guns, the crackle of rife-fire, distant cries and the whine of shells.

At about 2.15 on the morning of 9th May a Captain Scoular of No. 2 Company makes it back to Battalion HQ. He had entered Bulgarian trenches with part of his Company but they'd been bombed out. Among the three missing officers is Lieutenant Mitchell. Patrols sent out by the Royal Scots Fusiliers report that they can find no trace of the companies of the Scottish Rifles which had gone forward to the assault. In a day or two 'Missing' proves to be circumlocution for killed. Marshall Mitchell won't be going home to be man of the house for his 'mother-of-mine' and sisters at 211 West Princes Street. His holiday in Salonika is finished. God's will is clear on that point.

In due time Isa receives notification of the death of her son. She also receives an envelope containing his service medals, none suggesting any distinction. There isn't much scope for witnessed military distinction when you're despatched into mist. There's a citation from His Majesty's Government, what we would call a form letter. It presents its fulsome patriotic phrases in elegant printed calligraphy. At the end of the innumerably copied scroll a clerk has written the name in blood-red ink: 'Lieut. John Marshall Mitchell, Scottish Rifles'. The citation says:

> *He whom this scroll commemorates was numbered among those who, at the call of King and Country, left all that was dear to them, endured hardness, faced danger, and finally passed out of the sight of men by the path of duty and self-sacrifice, giving up their own lives that others might live in freedom.*
>
> *Let those who come after see to it that his name be not forgotten.*

***

Sibelius, what ideas can be crystallized from this delirium of bullets and lies? Can there be a kingdom of the big tune only in the dream-world of the artist? Is the Third Symphony just an aesthetic fiction? Could the assurance of its 'one and all-sufficing climax' take away the pain from Isa and her daughters? Is your popular, sad waltz closer to the truth than the élitist eloquence of the Symphony? Can the child's prayer hold its own with the grown-ups? Does it ever get an answer?

76

And what are we to make of Marshall's last letter? Is it unambiguously the letter of a patriot and Christian, a conformist who obeyed orders and went unquestioningly into battle for King and Country, grateful for the issue of sun helmets, food and sleep, readily surrendering his life to the judgement of his Battalion commander and the will of his God and dutifully signing off his loving but rather formal message with 'I have some Platoon work to do this afternoon, which won't bear delaying any longer'? If he could have written letter No. 2223 without the inhibition of censorship, would he have written differently? Would he have mentioned the fate of luckless Patrick Downey or the Transport Officer's lonely suicide, or the feet shattered by Mills grenades in the pockets of dead comrades?

Or would the letter have remained much the same because as man of the house his obligation is to comfort and reassure his widowed mother and three sisters? Is his reference to *Valse Triste* a coded way of telling them he expects to die soon but they should be calm because he's prepared for this and not afraid? When he passed from the sight of men in the reek of mist and explosives, when the Bulgarian shell or bayonet found him – or when he was caught in the obscene euphemism, 'friendly fire' – was there an atomic instant of epiphany when he saw the faces of home or felt the succour of his God?

Or was it not like that at all? Did death come with spectral tenderness, not the big tune but *Valse Triste* after all, taking him in its arms, dancing him away from the mockery of earthly perversities?

And who would grossly question Nora's memory of his valediction? His service medals have been buried with the Government's glib citation in a drawer of the sideboard used as a dumping ground for lifeless memorabilia. She sits alone in the blank inertia of bereavement while the half-light of dusk gathers in the living room at 211 West Princes Street. At the side of the bay window, to the right of the piano, he stands erect, crisply uniformed, capped and gloved as if ready for inspection or like a sentry on guard. There is no movement in his face but the eyes beckon. She rises from her chair and walks to him as the waltz begins its gravely spaced pizzicato chords and he raises his arms towards her. She can feel his hand through the leather glove and caresses his cheek with her own. His right hand on her waist guides her into the quickening spiral of the dance. Her feet are nimble, her heart sings and the room spins. Light fades with the dying fall of the music and he's gone. She sits again, at peace in the darkened room, her hand still conscious of his, her feet remembering.

3. Books and God

The Queen's Eye Specialist in Scotland was wrong. I didn't become a grocer and I didn't go blind. For reasons of its own the myopia stopped progressing and the fog lifted. There was a chance meeting between the eminent oculist and my father.

'Oh yes, your son – he was one of my mistakes', said the eminence, letting fifteen years of fumbling, dread and headaches go at that.

A royally branded mistake, I was leaving school with an inferiority complex and an appetite for literature perversely whetted, no doubt, by the limit put on reading during the years of accelerating myopia. Most of all there was music, especially yours, but no executant prowess. I had been allowed to take up your instrument, the violin, too late to achieve anything better than variations on 'The Vicar of Bray' crammed with arpeggios which sounded like Bartók in a bad temper, forebore to abuse the instrument further and stuck to the gramophone. A consequence of the amount of time I spent alone and motionless in its company was that, like the young Robert Louis Stevenson, I was 'known and pointed out for the pattern of an idler'.

After school the orthodox middle-class destination was university. It was also the obvious way to turn literature into a degree and a meal-ticket. Blackened by decades of urban pollution the University of Glasgow was a kenspeckle landmark across the city, grandiose and stylistically absurd. But now it had to be taken seriously as the workplace and arbiter of worth, Scotland's second university, modelled on the University of Bologna, founded in 1451, some forty years after the University of St Andrews. Originally based at Glasgow's medieval cathedral, it shifted to new buildings in the High Street in 1460, became

79

known as 'The Old College' and moved again in 1870 to its present home on the top of Gilmorehill designed by Sir George Gilbert Scott and capped by the tower added by his son, John Oldrid Scott. A school-leaver from the greater Glasgow area or the West of Scotland would most likely go here for further education, following the footsteps of the University's innumerable distinguished men and women. There was Francis Hutcheson, Professor of Moral Philosophy from 1729 until his death in 1746, breaking with tradition by lecturing in English as well as Latin and teaching Adam Smith for whom he was 'the never to be forgotten Dr Hutcheson'. His philosophy of benevolence helped stoke the fires of revolution in North America. There was William Thomson, Lord Kelvin, Professor of Natural Philosophy and arguably the pre-eminent scientist of the nineteenth century. There were James Watt of the steam engine and John Logie Baird, pioneer of television. There were stars of literature: James Boswell, Tobias Smollett, John Buchan and Catherine Carswell. There were John Grierson, father of the documentary, and the psychiatrist R. D. Laing. The English Department was currently headed by Professor Peter Alexander, probably the foremost Shakespearean scholar of the day. There were lectures by Edwin Morgan, then in his thirties, destined to become Glasgow and Scotland's first Poet Laureate. Scott Junior's grubby neo-Gothic spire was no longer an architectural joke. It was a towering rubric of minatory stone.

'Who do you think you are', it demanded, 'to be coming here into this constellation of geniuses?'

There could be no answer to that. I took a number 10 bus to University Avenue, psyched myself into the enrolment hall and signed on for English Literature, taking heart from the evident diffidence of others doing the same.

University of Glasgow

81

Anglo-Saxon poetry was life stripped of trivia. The elegiac stoicism of 'The Wanderer' endorsed my adolescent solitude; the icy-feathered tern called lurching testosterone to character-forming hazard on the gannet's bath with 'The Seafarer'. How well these sombre Nordic broodings would go with the weathers of your *En Saga,* Sibelius. Cliffs, sea-spray, howling winds and polar light.

To string arpeggios over a motif in bassoons and horns the dragon-prowed longship lifts and falls on the harbour wave, awaiting its crew and an out-going tide. Eager to be off, its timbers creak under the trading weight of silver and jewels, honey, pottery and leather. Horns proclaim the epic theme. Viking men settle to twenty pairs of oars, pulling the ship into open sea. Wind fills the great square sail. The tempo quickens from andante to allegro and the ship steers south. Through shrouds of sea-spray Shetland's black cliffs glower after the longship battling another fifty miles of wild ocean for landfall on Orkney. To a murmuring passage for strings a lovestruck sailor, missing his girl, carves his graffito on the wall of a Pictish burial mound: 'INGEBORG IS THE FAIREST OF WOMEN'. Time to brave the sea again as woodwind and a surge of strings call the crew back to oars and ocean. The wind rises. Oarsmen dig into hard water. After the white-capped swell of the Pentland Firth, west round the top of Scotland, south still, past islands of the Outer Hebrides, and down to Iona. The sailors beach on Columba's sacred isle but there's no berserking, no pillage. Bent not on plunder but discovery our Vikings rest on their oars to wonder at the roar of ocean punching into the isle of Staffa's great cave, Fingal's long before it was Mendelssohn's. When the dragon ship gets home there will be much to tell Ingeborg.

82

83

Fingal's Cave, Isle of Staffa.

84

Isle of Staffa

Of course Beatrix Potter had anticipated such heroic grapplings in The Tale of Mr Jeremy Fisher, her epic of the piscatorial frog who lives in a damp house among buttercups:

> *The water was all slippy-sloppy in the larder*
> *and in the back passage.*
> *But Mr Jeremy Fisher liked getting his feet*
> *wet; nobody ever scolded him, and he never*
> *caught a cold!*

What a stylist, Sibelius! Impeccable prose: lucid, expertly cadenced. Proper words in proper places illustrated by Potter's lyrical miniatures. It's all there. Poling his lily-leaf boat into the pond to fish for minnows, Mr Jeremy Fisher is Ulysses, Ishmael, Siegfried and your Lemminkäinen. A hostile world fires its warning shot when a water-beetle tweaks the toe of one of his galoshes as he lunches on a butterfly sandwich. Instead of a minnow for dinner he lands a pricking stickleback. (How often has that happened to us?) A shoal of little fish put their heads out of the water and laugh at Mr Jeremy Fisher. (Common, contemptible *Schadenfreude*.) He's snatched from his boat by a 'great big enormous trout' which carries him to the bottom of the pond but is so displeased with the taste of Mr Jeremy's macintosh that it spits him out, leaving the tattered, indomitable frog to hop home, dress his fingers with sticking plaster and serve roasted grasshopper to his classy chums, Mr Alderman Ptolemy Tortoise and Sir Isaac Newton. Mr Jeremy Fisher had come through.

In *Beowulf* my sympathies were all with Grendel, the cursed outcast, in his tormented hatred of whingeing Hrothgar and the mead-sodden hard men of Club Heorot. Chaucer was a wordy comic-book in language whose sole purpose was to give stone-faced morphologists and dialecticians – ovoid persons with lank hair and mossy teeth – a power trip, driving addled, panicking students to thoughts of sedition or suicide. Shakespeare was Boss, moralist supreme, top phrase-monger and subtle-souled psychologist, but how the professors lowered him into textual quibbles between the Quartos or down to the second best bed. Milton's God was a spiteful puppeteer, his Punch-and-Judy paradise well lost for Satan's 'courage never to submit or yield' and the pornographic cunning of his 'spirited sly snake'. Adam was what we called in unregenerate Scotland 'a big tumfy', i.e. a stodgy, obsequious conformist, and even then it was obvious that Eve's wide-eyed 'God is thy law, thou mine' would warrant the fire of combusting feminism, but despite my own lucky escape from the country of the blind I could still join in Samson's *cri de coeur*:

> ......*why was the sight*
> *To such a tender ball as th' eye confin'd,*
> *So obvious and so easie to be quencht,*
> *And not as feeling through all parts diffus'd,*
> *That she might look at will through every*
> > *pore?*

Jane Austen was still the authority on woman with nothing to fear from D.H. Lawrence's Lady C. or the rococo sexualities of Iris Murdoch. Pope was the complete sophisticate and Lord of the Epigram, Swift the excremental visionary and King of Spleen, springing one of literature's great surprises with his lapse into perfectly balanced tenderness when the Sorrel Nag bids banished Gulliver farewell from the country of the Houyhnhnms: 'Take care of thyself, gentle Yahoo'.

Nothing could damage Wordsworth's epiphanic 'spots of time' in *The Prelude*, not even his own leaden

87

philosophizing and Rousseauesque bucolic fantasy about the moral superiority of humble and rustic life. In 'Tintern Abbey' his 'glad animal movements' were always good for a snigger and he should have dropped the mushy apostrophe to sister Dorothy, but all was forgiven for the way he made you believe in

> *A motion and a spirit, that impels*
> *All thinking things, all objects of all thought,*
> *And rolls through all things*

which catered to the need for some sort of God, sang like an orchestra and chimed with what I felt about your music, Sibelius. You and Wordsworth were conspiring to save me from the arid securities of atheism, with some assistance from Robert Browning's savvy Bishop Blougram:

> *Just when we are safest, there's a sunset*
>   *touch,*
> *A fancy from a flower-bell, some one's death,*
> *A chorus-ending from Euripides, —*
> *And that's enough for fifty hopes and fears*
> *As old and new at once as Nature's self,*
> *To rap and knock and enter in our soul,*
> *Take hands and dance there, a fantastic ring,*
> *Round the ancient idol, on his base again, —*
> *The grand Perhaps!*

Dickens wasn't much in fashion then, so my beloved *Great Expectations* and *Bleak House* were safe from the critical slings and arrows of academe. Pip remained intact as the model hero, gutted by love, manipulated by money, indoctrinated by snobbery, finally processed to redemption by the fruitiest characters in the Dickens pantheon. George Eliot ended *Middlemarch* with the noblest prose sentence in Eng. Lit., appealing to my heartfelt if unstructured egalitarianism:

*...for the growing good of the world is partly
dependent on unhistoric acts; and that
things are not so ill with you and me as
they might have been, is half owing to the
number who lived faithfully a hidden life,
and rest in unvisited tombs.*

Maybe a strong sense of underlying equality is genetically part of the Scottish idiom. Expressed as 'the sons of Adam', the idea of a common humanity beyond hierarchical accident or political manoeuvring is a liberal fancy (not that it's tempting to think of Adam as Dad), but the Scottish expression that we're all 'Jock Tamson's bairns' asserts equality in terms of a continuing, imaginable family under a knowable flesh-and-blood 'faither'. Death the leveller is tamed to assuasive inevitability by the song in *Cymbeline* which accepts that 'the sceptre, learning, physic' must, like golden lads, girls and chimney-sweepers, 'come to dust'; but Charles Murray's Scots poem, 'A Green Yule', hammers home a grittier *memento mori* about the equalizing reality of a common end without the anaesthetizing balm of Shakespeare's consolatory music. It's tough, it's true and very Scottish:

*Dibble them doon, the laird, the loon,
  King an' the cadgin caird,
The lady fine beside the queyn,
  A' in the same kirkyaird.*

*The warst, the best, they a' get rest;
  Ane 'neath a headstane braw,
Wi' deep-cut text, while ower the next
  The wavin' grass is a'.*

*Mighty o' name, unknown to fame,
  Slippit aneth the sod;*

Greatest an' least alike face east,
Waitin' the trump o' God.

With Wilfred Owen I moved my slaughtered uncle into the sun, railed at fatuous sunbeams for failing to resurrect him and gave thanks for *Valse Triste*'s mystic visitation to grieving Nora. James Joyce was a new horizon when he recorded the minutiae of the mind's inner workings in *Ulysses*, but mostly an elephantine bore in *Finnegans Wake* – literature's prankster, tone-row Schoenberg – playing intricate language games like an obsessional schoolboy in an attic with a fancy train set only he knew how to operate. Admittedly he could turn on moments of enchanting music like the pun on the Lord´s Prayer in his hymn to the River Liffey:

...haloed be her eve, her singtime sung, her
rill be run, unhemmed as it is uneven!

In *The Waste Land* T.S. Eliot made a paradigm of twentieth-century *angst* and brought freedom from literalism. Here was poetry working full throttle in an idiom for the times, each line a struck tuning-fork resonating into the next, even if some of the lines weren't quite his own and his unreal cities were so many sanitized, mandarin miles away from the real grime of post-war Glasgow. There was a whole song in the first two lines of 'Gerontion':

Here I am, an old man in a dry month,
Being read to by a boy, waiting for rain.

The lines throbbed with implication, rhythmically pointed by the impeccably judged hiatus, the intake of breath between 'boy' and 'waiting'. A musician's trick, Sibelius, which you would relish. Then came his allusion to battles of Thermopylae and the hacking cutlass of a later age:

> *I was neither at the hot gates*
> *Nor fought in the warm rain*
> *Nor knee deep in the salt marsh, heaving a*
>   *cutlass,*
> *Bitten by flies, fought.*

Writing the poem in 1919 he could have said, 'I did not see action on the Somme'. After 1944 he could have said, 'I was not at Omaha Beach'. He wasn't there, yet on an imaginative level he knew the agonies of both, making us feel them too in the syncopating tremor of his second hiatus between 'flies' and 'fought'. This is the rhetoric of rhythmic spacing you use at the end of your Fifth Symphony. It was Eliot's imagery of alienation, of course, which readied us for the 'nothing is funnier than unhappiness' of Samuel Beckett's tramps and Harold Pinter's 'weasel in the cocktail cabinet'. The critics pressed on students by the professors in fat Roneoed bibliographies were occasionally visited for silent conversation, an hour in a library with one of their books after unmediated engagement with the poem, play or fiction. Unfortunately the professors seemed more interested in what we thought about the critics than our response to the literature or the connection between literature and life. Some of them didn't seem to have done much living.

Writers were brain surgeons. Even unlikeable writers contributed to the lift of consciousness and appraisal of existence in relation to values because of the case we were obliged to make for disliking them. I tended to agree with George Orwell that there's something fraudulent about literary criticism, that literary judgements trump up a personal set of rules to support subjective preferences. Similarly with judgements of music. The 'happening to us' of a work of art tends to beggar understanding and you will have realized by now, Sibelius, that a junky is no critic. The British writer, George Steiner, confesses that 'the opening bass, the hammer-beat of Edith Piaf's "Je ne regrette rien"' tempt all his nerves, drawing him into 'God knows what infidelities to reason' each time he hears it played. I would swap the whole of Verdi for Sinatra singing 'I've got you under my skin', surely the most pornographic of popular songs.

'No man or woman need justify his or her personal anthology, his canonic welcomes', says Steiner. 'Love does not argue its necessities'.

A stout British empirical tradition is there to support Steiner, notably in Dr Johnson for whom, 'in questions that relate to the heart of man', the ultimate arbiter is 'the common voice of the multitude, uninstructed by precept and unprejudiced by authority'.

It's open to anyone to love 'Valse Triste' and remain closed to your 'major' works. The popular waltz will always speak to people who would run a mile from a symphony concert, but popularity can't diminish its perfect realization of what it intends to say. Yet despite portentous intellectualizing of Pop Art, earnest readings of popular films and the twilight zone between high and lower brows dimly charted by some Beatles' songs, Stephen Sondheim's grittier musicals and the operas of John Adams and Philip Glass, a sturdy if vaguely based complacency about the distinction between serious and popular has persisted. In Britain this complacency survived The Who's 1969 flirtation with opera in *Tommy*, subsequently adapted for Broadway by Pete Townshend to thrill 'audiences of responsible American forty-somethings with its energy and hit-power'. It survived Pink Floyd's bids for the grandiose in their 'concept' albums, but trembled when Nigel Kennedy repackaged himself and Pavarotti filled the stage in Hyde Park, performing in the open air like the supergroups. In America Madonna was disconcertingly appointed vice-president of the Institute of Contemporary Arts. Philip Glass composed his 'Low' Symphony, reworking material from a 1975 rock album by David Bowie and Brian Eno. The English National Opera launched 'New Visions, New Voices', a project open to anyone under 30 who wants to 'do' opera, applicants to the scheme being encouraged to use their own preferred forms of music, whether house music, heavy metal or plain old pop. Ivory towers were crumbling and cultural uniforms shedding their insignia in this jumbling of categories, with the producer in charge of 'New Visions, New Voices', saying that he would be happier 'if people turned up to a first night at the English National Opera in jeans, rather than the furs and diamonds that make my heart sink'. Culture, as it doggedly continued to be even when Malinowski redefined it to mean the material and mental habitat of a people, was pushing out from behind the red ropes of the museum.

Then came a symphony from Poland in which 'serious' and 'popular' appeared to coincide. We heard a musical setting of a prayer inscribed by an eighteen year-old girl on wall 3 of cell no. 3 in the basement of 'Palace', the Gestapo headquarters in Zakopane, Poland:

> *No, Mother, do not weep,*
> *Most chaste Queen of Heaven*
> *Support me always.*
> *'Zdrowas Mario' ['Ave Maria'].*

The tragic graffito gave Henryk Górecki the text for the second movement of his Symphony No 3, subtitled the 'Symphony of Sorrowful Songs'. Composed in 1976, first performed the following year to a mixed reception, Górecki's symphony was recorded twice and gained a small following. In 1992 it was recorded again by the London Sinfonietta conducted by David Zinman with the American soprano Dawn Upshaw. Each of its three movements centres on a text of harrowing sorrow. First there is a fifteenth-century Polish prayer known as the Holy Cross Lament which is the voice of the Mother of God talking to Christ: 'My son, my chosen and beloved/Share your wounds with your mother'; the third movement sets a folk song of the Opolskiego, in which a mother laments the death of her son, killed during an uprising. The music is marked 'Lento' throughout and, as you said of your Fourth Symphony, Sibelius, 'there is nothing of the circus' about it. In June 1992 the distributor, Warner Music, announced the sale of 300,000 copies with the work reaching No. 1 in the UK and USA classical music charts and simultaneously achieving No. 6 in the British Pop charts. Since then sales have apparently risen well above 500,000. So the symphony became both a 'serious' and 'popular' cultural phenomenon in America and Britain. When the disc was first released critics were tentatively favourable. Then they massed to the attack: 'A load of gloomy piffle' (Alexander Waugh in *Evening Standard*); 'There is less to this music than meets the ear' (David Mellor in *The Guardian*); 'Why this really rather dreary symphony has sent all those people into the record shops baffles me' (Michael Kennedy in *The Sunday Telegraph*); 'Henryk Górecki seems a very nice man, and it is because of perverse resentment of its popularity that I do not possess the now famous recording of his third symphony' (Stephen Pettit in *The Times*).

This last comment is the most revealing. It begins with condescension – 'Henryk Górecki is a very nice man' – and then comes clean: the critic hasn't bought a copy of the recording because he resents the work's popularity. His admission that the resentment is perverse amounts to a substantial critical concession, implying that popularity taints though it shouldn't, that serious music-lovers can't help being snobs, and that they are at fault for putting élitism before art. He offers the proposition that the popularity of a work is, axiomatically, sufficient ground for rejecting it and, above all, admits that this is wrong. But wrong or not, and despite examples like *Uncle Tom's Cabin*, *Doctor Zhivago*, Beethoven's Fifth Symphony and *West Side Story*, these responses to the Górecki symphony imply that the periphery is where the popular permanently belongs.

The success of Górecki's work has been attributed to marketing, an explanation which fails to take account of the kind of object for sale. It has been suggested that people use the symphony as New Age wallpaper or musical Mogadon, but who is easily tranquillized by the intensity of grief the music expresses? Perhaps, then, we must wonder at the popularity of a work which speaks of primary things, of mother and son, love, victimization and loss, and, finally, the possibility of redemption; which, like Keneally and Spielberg's Schindler, teaches us anew how to weep for Auschwitz, for Bosnia and Darfur and, in doing this, melts cultural boundaries to the benefit of all and the aesthetic, psychological, perhaps even spiritual credit of some 500,000 people. The appeal of this work to people on both sides of the line formerly supposed to divide serious from popular may be one of the best hopes we have had for some time. We want more art like this.

Analysis can reveal the craftsmanship of your symphonies and show how your manipulation of form develops from the First to the Seventh, but no analysis can prove that my addiction to your music instead of Mozart's, Bruckner's or Gershwin's is warranted or not. Aesthetic concepts of proportion, development and integration can be used to justify your revision of the Fifth Symphony towards its most coherent form, but nothing can prove that the final version of 1919 is superior to the first of 1915 in some absolute sense because the first says different things. And nobody who loves the familiar 1919 version could wish to be without the enlarged awareness of your full range of feelings and ideas which a comparison of the two versions makes available. It's a pity that so little remains of the second version of 1916.

Probably it's more useful to talk about your affinity with the climate and landscapes of Finland and my love for the island of Lismore and the northwest of Scotland. We're both northerners and we've both found in the natural features of our places 'thoughts that do often lie too deep for tears'. Sometimes it seems as if they were the same thoughts, though it took your genius to voice them. Let's sit on this rock at the northern tip of Lismore. Blending with the cries of gulls a clarinet ruminates over soft timpani, the beginning of your First Symphony. The day is still. Below us the placid gloss of sea is broken only by cormorants coming up from a dive and the gruffly spluttering heads of seals. Look north, up the rift valley sculpted by glaciers to form the Great Glen of Scotland. To the east, you can see Ben Nevis just before its summit is wreathed in cloud and the thoughtful clarinet is answered by a power surge of strings. Your First Symphony is pacing down the Great Glen towards us with gusts of brass tone as

97

Ben Nevis

the wind rises. A pair of flutes over a background of strings and harp recalls us to our pastoral island and its playful seals before the pacing resumes and takes on speed. Soon your Symphony will be here beside us on our rock. Listen, Big Man, look, here it comes.

I must hand it to literature for defining my relationship to you. There's a famous poem called 'Anecdote of the Jar' by the American, Wallace Stevens. He published it in 1923 so you might have seen it in translation:

> *I placed a jar in Tennessee,*
> *And round it was, upon a hill.*
> *It made the slovenly wilderness*
> *Surround that hill.*

The humanly manufactured jar is art which is different from nature's 'bird or bush'. 'Tennessee' could just as easily be Rannoch Moor, Africa, the Karelia or anywhere. Nature, the 'wilderness', is random and without order until the unnatural jar is brought into it. Then the jar takes dominion, everything refers to it and is 'no longer wild' because the jar confers order on what had been 'slovenly', formless matter. You were my jar in Tennessee, Sibelius, the point of reference whereby life's disparate pieces might be collated into a shape. Anyone who can't find a god should be sure to pick a jar. Better to have both.

***

'How a man can get along without religion I can't understand', you said, Sibelius. 'Life is full of enigmas, and the older I grow the more I perceive how precious little we actually know. The fact that man believes and always has believed in God, proves in my opinion that a higher Being rules all that is – how and in what form we cannot naturally know'.

It was easy enough to agree with you about enigmas and the history of belief in divinity, not so easy to accept an unknowable higher Being with any interest in us lot. Given the hells on earth humankind has been permitted to construct, it was next to impossible to suppose that such a Being cared much what people did to each other. What about the fate of children in times of racial persecution and ethnic cleansing or natural disaster? Could the hunger for God be proof of his existence? Not by analogy. A person might be lost in the desert, parched and starving, but hunger for steak and chips and cold beer wouldn't make them real.

Sarastro's prayer to Isis and Osiris in *The Magic Flute* has been called the only music which could, without blasphemy, be put into the mouth of God. That reduced God to a portly bass in a tuneful pantomime. Your symphonies had Sarastro knocked cold. They gave your belief in a higher Being an authority beyond both theological argument and personal testimony. Whatever higher essence you'd made contact with was speaking through you in the music; it wasn't just you talking about it in the way Beethoven talks about brotherhood in the Ninth Symphony or Shostakovich about war and tyranny in the 'Leningrad'.

God wasn't a problem in early childhood. My father's omniscience was confirmed by his intimacy with the Lord he always thanked in the grace he said at mealtime, a short conversation which, if one-sided, took amiable divine attention for granted. Bedtime prayers for the well-being of loved ones were a daily reminder that the Lord was listening. The Episcopalian Church broke this short-lived security.

At first the Sunday morning services were like big parties. In time of war it was comforting to see so many grown-ups doing the same thing, singing and praying together, and it was cosy to sit snug and safe between my parents. My father's Sunday jacket was made of Harris tweed which had a distinctive smell like mixed herbs. He sang with his heart and soul:

'O all ye Works of the Lord, bless ye the Lord: praise him, and magnify him for ever'.

The smell of his jacket seemed to get stronger when he sang. I thought this must be what God smelled like. Then everyone listened to a speech by the man they called the Vicar. It was his party. There was always a bit of the party when he asked us to pray for the sick. I thought this was very kind and prayed fervently for people I'd never seen or heard of before.

'Please, God, make poor Mr Thomson's bronchitis go away and mend Miss Newton's sore legs'.

The parties stopped being enjoyable when I began to understand the words better. Kneeling between my mother and father I heard their confessions as if for the first time.

'Almighty and most merciful Father', they murmured into clasped hands, 'We have erred and strayed from thy ways like lost sheep. We have followed too much the devices and desires of our own hearts. We have offended against thy holy laws. We have left undone those things which we ought to have done, and we have done those things which we ought not to have done, and there is no health in us'.

This was shattering. I knew my father's health was questionable because I'd learned that he was called 'diabetic' and watched him injecting medicine into his thigh; but my mother was visibly fit and strong. I'd seen her carry three shopping bags, one in each hand

and a third in her teeth. Now they were telling God they were sick, lost sheep and miserable offenders. Parental omnipotence and infallibility were shot. I had been deceived.

For a lad born out of wedlock Jesus had done well. He never seemed to have been bothered about his illegitimacy and he'd devised an admirable manual for the moral life, apart from the injunction to turn the other cheek and his assurance that the meek would inherit the earth, which was obviously the opposite of what went on in the world. If we'd all been meek Hitler would have conquered us and our Jewish people would have been gassed. God lost it when it emerged that he'd made Mary pregnant while she belonged to Joseph and refused to stop his son being crucified, installing pain at the centre of Christianity. Sleaze and treachery were no attributes for a higher Being. Then the Vicar told us Mr Thomson had died of his bronchitis.

No more Sunday parties for me, Sibelius. My father was angry. He had failed in his duty to bring me up as a Christian. My mother was sad. I tried to palliate their disappointment by calling myself an agnostic instead of an atheist, but didn't really know what I was. My father told me I'd believe in God if I was ever lucky enough to win the love of a woman as good as my mother. That was going to take some time.

Hunger for God gnawed on. I confessed it to a Presbyterian minister.

'Life without Jesus Christ is like lamb without mint sauce', he said.

My favourite graffito was scrawled on a pillar of one of the massive concrete overpasses in the Los Angeles freeway system. 'Nietzsche is dead, signed God' read the message supposedly spray-painted by a heavenly aerosol which, no doubt, scrupled to use no fluorocarbon. The popularity of Steven Spielberg's *Close Encounters of the Third Kind* and *E.T.* depended on an atavistic yearning for something godlike from beyond the stars, a longing powerful enough to dispose of any requirement that the supreme Being, if visible, need be anything much to look at. God as a bug-eyed caterpillar who could make a bicycle fly would do fine if that was the best offer going. A cute God sorted better with the commercial taste of the times than the doubtful beneficence of a heavenly Father with a 'raft' of prohibitions. My graffito appeared to be what the purveyor of hot money calls 'a non-consecutive oncer'. Even without Nietzsche's help God seemed to be dead all right, harried to vanishing point by Shelley and his friend Thomas Jefferson Hogg in 1811, zapped from behind by Darwin and Huxley, vaporized by Freud, savaged by Marx and Lenin, discredited by association with British imperialist jingoism, rumbled by relativity, excoriated by D.H. Lawrence, bound and gagged by logical positivism, tortured by Graham Greene and deep-sixed not only by Nietzsche but repeatedly by economics or, as God would have put it, Mammon. Neither the zealous politicizing of a jet-setting Pope, nor competing styles of holy-rolling, nor the militancy of sectarian Islam held out much prospect of an agreeable second coming. It would be a rough beast indeed, as Yeats imagined, that would slouch towards Bethlehem to be born of our *zeitgeist*.

Yet the sense of loss persisted. However austere he was in his time, however prohibitive, however psychologically damaging and divisive, however unacceptable to a child whose parents had been changed into lost sheep, he was included still in many toasts to absent friends. In the process of being westernized Salman Rushdie lost his Muslim faith.

102

'When I was young I was religious in quite an unthinking way', he said. 'Now I'm not, but I am conscious of a space where God was'.

Me too. But then we heard nine million children in Africa have lost a mother to Aids, 1.2 million Indian children die every year because of malnutrition and 5.6 million children die every year from malnutrition-linked causes. Isn't this pushing the 'sins of the father' formula a little far? What kind of higher Being lets this happen, Sibelius? I'll grant you inscrutable, but what are *you* going to do about it, God? Let's face it, wouldn't it be callous to believe in you? Where is the grace of your purpose here? Where were you at Dachau, Auschwitz, Treblinka? Where are you now in Darfur? After a hellish journey to Birkenau in 1944 Elie Wiesel saw Jewish babies thrown into a flaming ditch.

'Never shall I forget the small faces of the children whose bodies I saw transformed into smoke under a silent sky...Never shall I forget those moments that murdered my God and my soul and turned my dreams to ashes'.

I remained suspended, as the God of George Herbert's 'The Pulley' would have me, 'in repining restlessness', missing my father's Harris tweed jacket and the green smell of mixed herbs.

4. The Clinic and Mr Whyte

After four years I said good-bye to the University's constellation of geniuses, my ordinariness confirmed, and left with an MA and gratitude for mental furniture I wouldn't have had the wit to collect otherwise. But there had been a price. I'd had to give up my daily fix of Sibelius. You were too much The Big Man; my jar had too much dominion.

When reading for the degree began I realised that I couldn't listen to your music and focus on the book of the moment or the essay on *The Faerie Queene* due to be handed to my tutor in a fortnight, or the aggressions of end-of-term exams. I even had to find a way not to be distracted by the importunacies of remembered music or else be lost to the printed page for hours on end.

Without conscious invitation or apparent cause the shimmer of muted strings that begins your Violin Concerto was transport to Lismore where the reeds of Loch Fiart whisper their island secrets. Like Mendelssohn's Violin Concerto yours begins without introductory flourish, giving the impression that the music has been playing before we've begun to hear it and I sit again with my father in the brown rowing-boat looking across the rings of rising trout towards the flank of the Bàrr Mòr, speckled with lambs. When the violin reaches out into the harmony of water, hill and sky, yearning to belong, the orchestra meets the need, receiving the solo voice into itself. Again the violin sings in an ecstasy of longing and suddenly the soloist is a bird climbing the air, then winging down into a full-throated response from the orchestra. This is the core not only of this movement but of the whole Concerto. Implicit in it are both the elegiac serenity of the second movement and the exuberance of the third which Sir Donald Tovey called 'a polonaise for polar bears'. But this last movement is not entirely extrovert. Just before the last resolving chords the violin remembers the intensities of the first two movements. This is affirmation in a world of continuing questions and I have forgotten the book in my hand.

Literature couldn't compete with you. Sibelius heard in the morning was a pre-emptive strike for possession of the day's consciousness. Sibelius heard in the evening flared into the mind next morning. I had to practice suppression, self-denial. You had to be exiled to silence until the work of literature was done, the degree achieved and I was qualified to look for a job.

So I committed myself to a phantom clinic where music was prohibited. There was a big sign at the entrance: 'NO COMPOSERS, ESPECIALLY IF YOU'RE SIBELIUS'. The clinic was policed by Literature which sent its creatures to mock my self-denial.

Prancing from bed to bed on his morning round the offensively merry Registrar, Dr Joseph Addison, told me what I was missing. He threw me a jaunty couplet.

'Music, the greatest good that mortals know,
And all of heaven we have below'.

'Fine, okay', I said, 'but I'm absenting myself from felicity awhile'.

'If music be the food of love, play on', simpered Dr Orsino, a cruisey locum from the Illyrian Infirmary. A copy of *Twelfth Night* protruded from the pocket of his white medical coat. There was a picture of him on the cover, languidly sprawled beside a huge gramophone.

'Oh, belt up, lover boy', I said, 'You know I can't listen to music and read you at the same time. Get back inside your play'.

The male nurse was Cockney, name of Keats.

'Heard melodies are sweet', he chirped, adjusting my pillows, 'but those unheard are sweeter'.

'Maybe that's all you think you need to know', I rejoined, 'but you've never heard a tune by The Big Man'.

The Welsh cleaning lady was a Mrs Organ Morgan from Llareggub under Milk Wood.

'Oh, I'm a martyr to music', she cried, flailing her mop under my bed.

'Me too, lady', I groaned.

A bearded gentleman seemed to be the ward's head doctor. He had an Irish accent and looked at me with very beady eyes.

'Music', he snapped, 'is the brandy of the damned'.

'All right, Dr Shaw', I said, 'and I've been on the wagon since I came to this place, so push off'.

Hardest to take was the sanctimonious psychotherapist, Dr Lorenzo, a willowy Venetian, who scolded me in pompous blank verse.

> 'The man that hath no music in himself,
> Nor is not moved with concord of sweet
>   sounds,
> Is fit for treasons, stratagems and spoils;
> The motions of his spirit are dull as night,
> And his affections dark as Erebus,
> Let no such man be trusted'.

'U-huh, take your point, Doc', I said, 'couldn't agree more. I've got plenty of music in me, that's why I'm here. This *is* a stratagem to avoid the distraction of sweet sounds until I've got my degree, and your therapy stinks'.

'I know your stops', quipped Hamlet, whizzing through the ward, his doublet all unbraced.

'And I've got an essay to write about yours for Tuesday', I called after him, 'how about a few clues?' But he was gone.

'So here it is', rumbled Mr Henry James, the American plastic surgeon with scalpels in his eyes, 'here's the special case'. He was a little flushed from nipping and tucking his *Portrait of a Lady*. 'Here's a young man the squareness of whose jaw bespeaks a want of easy consonance with the deeper rhythms of life'.

'Get away from my jaw', I grunted, 'my consonance is merely in abeyance until I've read the rest of you'.

That pleased him. He smiled complacently and vanished. I read the rest of him, graduated and discharged myself from the clinic.

***

Graduation meant I could come back to you, Sibelius. What piece of music would break the fast? The wireless chose for me. We called it a radio now. The brown commander of the living room which brought Ex. 19 had been replaced by a plastic box with perspex knobs and an illuminated turquoise dial inviting us to listen to Hilversum, Reykjavik and Luxembourg. Helsinki was tantalizingly there too but delivered only banshee whistles and static. Britannia still ruled the airwaves so once again it's the BBC I have to thank for ending my self-imposed abstinence with a broadcast performance of *Night Ride and Sunrise*.

The announcer said you wanted to convey the feelings of an ordinary man riding through dark forests towards dawn and the joyful sight of sunrise.

But the music probably also reflects your own fretful progress through fear of cancer, some 14 operations to remove a throat tumour and the sense of life renewed when the tumour was pronounced benign. With the histrionic egoism of youth I made my own profane story for the music. The 'Night Ride' section really describes the withdrawal shakes of a Sibelius addict who quits his junk cold turkey; 'Sunrise' is the well-being that builds in his veins with the first hit when he's back on his habit.

*****

Then Ian Whyte died. I hadn't seen him at all during the clinic time. News that he was in hospital with only a few months to live was both a shock and a reproach for my neglect of such a generous mentor. The BBC aunt had introduced me to him when I was keeping my eyes closed as much as possible in obedience to the eminent oculist and listening shut-eyed to all the music I could get. He had promptly invited me to attend his broadcast concerts at the BBC in Glasgow where I was often conspicuously an audience of one sitting at the back of the big studio. When the red light went out at the end of a broadcast, he'd call me over to the podium.

'How are you, boy? What have you been listening to?'

I had begun to keep notes about the music I heard on the wireless as well as performance details of my slowly growing treasure of recordings so I'd be ready for these welcome interrogations.

'Remember to choose records by Toscanini', he said, 'because he's always faithful to the score'. My earliest notion of good musical taste was shaped by Mr Whyte's nods, smiles and frowns. And Toscanini.

'Bach, Mozart and Brahms are the greatest musicians', he said, 'and Beethoven is the greatest poet. Then came Sibelius'.

So you always got a special nod and smile. He was a prolific composer himself, drawing on the Scottish vernacular tradition. Some 600 works in manuscript were collected after his death, including four symphonies, many arrangements of Scottish airs, an Oboe Concerto intended for Leon Goosens, a Violin Concerto once hailed by Max Rostal as 'the most significant this century' after yours, Sibelius, and the music for *Donald of the Burthens*, the ballet Leonide Massine choreographed for Covent Garden in 1951. Introducing bagpipes to an otherwise conventional score was the innovation which made this Whyte's best-known music. By remodelling a set of pipes to play at concert pitch he could bring them into his finale for a lively version of the *Reel of Tulloch*.

'Music is rather like a rippling burn', he said. 'It has its birth in high places and runs for the delight and benefit of all mankind. A German stream is naturally different from a Scottish burn – but everyone recognizes that water is the common element'.

'Mr Whyte, I'm having trouble with Prokofiev', I confessed.

'Why, boy?'

'Well, I like his music, but he uses so many discords'.

'Come with me', he said and led me to his spartan office with its very grand piano.

'Now what´s this, boy?' he said, playing a half-a-dozen bars of music.

'Beethoven's Fifth, sir', I said, grateful that he had chosen such an identifiable piece.

'Right, boy, and that', he said, striking a spread of keys in the sequence, 'is a discord. If Beethoven can

110

Ian Whyte, founder of the BBC Scottish Orchestra
Photograph kindly supplied by the BBC Scottish Symphony Orchestra © BBC

do it, so can Prokofiev. Don't worry about discords. They're part of music'.

So I stopped worrying.

***

The tall woman who got off the bus before me at the gates of Canniesburn hospital seemed familiar, but I couldn't place her at first. I followed her up the path to the cancer building where they'd given Mr Whyte a room to himself. It was dark, nearly 7 pm when visiting hour began at the hospital. I held my present for Mr Whyte, a biography of Toscanini by Howard Taubman, under my raincoat for protection from the December drizzle. When the woman paused in the lighted vestibule and turned to speak to a nurse I saw that she was Patricia Henderson, the studio announcer for Mr Whyte's concerts. People said she was his mistress and called her 'the red-light woman' which made her exotic and dangerous. Embarrassed, I turned to go but too late.

'Hello', she said, 'I know you don't I? You're the young man who used to sit at the back of the studio. Have you come to see Ian?'

'Oh, no, Miss Henderson, thank you, I wouldn't intrude, but could you please give this to him', I said, holding out the book, 'with my best wishes?'

'You must give it to him yourself', she said. 'He'd like that much better. On you go down that corridor. His room's the second one on the left. I'll wait here while you talk to him. Don't tell him I'm here. I'll come in a little while'.

The bed was opposite the door. Mr Whyte's head and shoulders were propped up on pillows and his hands were folded in front of him. His eyes looked out from a face of startling pallor towards the door,

112

watching for his lover, but graciously showing no disappointment when I entered instead.

'Come in, boy', he said. 'Bring that chair in beside the bed where I can see you'.

I gave him Toscanini.

'The Maestro', he said. 'Very kind of you, boy', and, as if there had been no break in our association, 'now what have you been listening to?'

'Last week I heard Sibelius's First Symphony for the first time'. It was true. The Second and Third were close friends by now but a composer's new arrivals are never chronological.

'Ah', he smiled, 'the First, where the journey starts. How lucky you are'.

***

The journey had really begun seven years before the First Symphony. Sibelius, if you hadn't been so precociously self-critical the First would have been your Second. 'A volcanic eruption', one observer called the scene in Helsinki University's Centennial Hall when you premièred the cantata *Kullervo Symphony* for soprano, baritone, male chorus and orchestra.

'It was like something that I had known for a long time and heard before', said a member of the chorus, 'It was Finnish music'.

It was Finnish language too, thanks to the text you took from the epic songs Elias Lönrott had welded into the unified text of the *Kalevala* to give Finland a mythical history rooted in the lore of its people. The *Kalevala* imbued Finnish national consciousness with a fresh, vital spirit empowered by a new sense of the past. Acclaim for the *Kullervo Symphony* was also vote of confidence in Finnish mythology, the Finnish language and a Finnish future. The Swedish language had dominated your culture for centuries.

113

Now it was in retreat. In a small way, Sibelius, Scots can identify with this. If you'd you picked up almost any British or Commonwealth newspaper in the first week of July 1999 you'd have read something like this. Let's face it, music, with the right words, had done it again:

Scotland makes royal faces burn

The royal family was subjected to an embarrassing moment during the opening of Scotland's new Parliament, enduring an emotional rendition of a song that mocks royalty.

As the Queen, the Duke of Edinburgh and Prince Charles sat stony-faced in front of the 129-member body, Scottish folk singer Sheena Wellington performed Robert Burns's socialist anthem, 'A Man's A Man for A' That'.

The song, which marked the highlight of the opening ceremony and was chosen by the organisers instead of Britain's national anthem, 'God Save the Queen', hails the nobility of honest poverty and pokes fun at the titles and trappings of nobility.

To members of Britain's nobility, the song was a slap in the face to the royal family.

'By choosing this song and rejecting the national anthem, they are flaunting a sort of separatism in a Parliament which is supposed to preserve the United Kingdom', the Earl of Lauderdale said.

In an emotional twist, all 129 new members of the Scottish Parliament loudly joined in for the last verse, which proclaims that a day will come

```
when 'over all the earth' men will
become brothers.
    Donald   Dewar,   Scotland's   First
Minister, added in an ensuing speech:
'At the heart of the song is a very
Scottish conviction that honesty and
simple dignity are priceless virtues,
not   imparted   by   rank   or   birth   or
privilege but part of the soul'.
```

The parallel here is the use of a song in the Scots language by Scotland's national bard to open a Parliament presided over by the English queen. At the time of *Kullervo*, like other Fennomen, you were trying to do away with traditional rank and privilege and cultural élitism in the drive to lift Finnish self-esteem above middle-to-upper class Swedish-speaking conformities which diluted truly Finnish national pride even though Swedish was your own first language and you never lost your fondness for it or your pleasure in speaking it. From the Finnish point of view, if you accept the parallel, the Earl of Lauderdale was the voice of Sweden. You Finns did much better than us Scots. After nearly 300 years of English rule we got our Parliament back with limited powers, but our Scots language has never become quite respectable. Despite the successes of the poets, Ramsay, Fergusson, and Burns, Scots was a threatened language for a long time after 1707 when the Act of Union installed English as the official language of Scotland, now part of the United Kingdom. Standard southern English soon became the language written by Scots people who wished to appear cultivated even if they still spoke their native Scots in informal situations. The most significant communication was now with London. Scots who visited the capital didn't want to be thought bumpkins because of their outlandish speech. On her journey through northern England in *The Heart of Midlothian* Sir Walter Scott's Jeanie Deans replaces her tartan screen with an English-style bonnet but is made to suffer for her language:

> *...her accent and language drew down on her so many jests and gibes, couched in a worse patois by far than her own, that she soon found it was her interest to talk as little and as seldom as possible.*

The language of government was the language of civilization even if poets thought differently and the natural use of dialect was still unacceptable in turn-of-the-century Scottish classrooms. In William McIlvanney's novel, *Docherty*, young Conn Docherty's teacher asks the boy what's wrong with his face:

> *'Skint ma nose, sur'.*
> *'How?'*
> *'Ah fell an' bumped ma heid in the sheuch [gutter], sur'.*
> *'I beg your pardon?'*
> *'Ah fell an' bumped ma heid in the sheuch, sur'.*
> *'I beg your pardon?'*
> *In the pause Conn understands the nature of the choice, tremblingly, compulsively, makes it.*
> *'Ah fell an' bumped ma heid in the sheuch, sur'.*
> *The blow is instant.*
> *'That, Docherty, is impertinence. You will translate, please, into the mother-tongue'.*

Standard English couldn't outlaw the Scots vernacular any more than Swedish could suppress spoken Finnish. In 1993 The Scottish Language Centre was proud to affirm the language's persistence:

*In spite o twa hunner year o Standart English
bein learnt in the schules the lenth an breadth
o Scotland – aw ye need tae dae is tae keep yer
lugs cockit an ye'll hear that Scots is still aboot,
whither ye're argyin in Ayr or Aiberdeenshire,
bidin in Buckie or Biggar, crackin in Castlemilk
or Crieff or daunderin roon Dumbarton or
Dundee.*

True, but we never achieved the respectability for
Scots that you did for Finnish. When we use the Scots
of our upbringing, people still look at us queerly, as if
they can see wee tartan gonks grimacing behind our
words, or as if they think we're just trying to be cute.
Havers, Sibelius, we're just being ourselves.

It's clear that you're talking about the Finnish
soul in the *Kullervo Symphony*. The puzzle is your
selection of material from the *Kalevala*, most of all
your choice of Kullervo, a hero as doomed as Oedipus.
There were many vivid characters to choose from.
You might have picked the figure of Väinämöinen, the
ageless singer who plants the barren earth, invents
the harp called the *kantele* and saves the people
from famine and pestilence. Another candidate
was Ilmarinen, the eternal smith and forger of the
talismanic Sampo, personification of the Finnish work
ethic. Another was Lemminkäinen, the embodiment
of erotic love, whose story you would tell later in the
Four Legends from the Kalevala. Instead you chose a
tragic youth persecuted by Untamo, his murderous
uncle who has apparently killed his family. Kullervo
is sold into slavery under Ilmarinen and put to work
as a herdsman. After taking revenge on Ilmarinen's
malicious wife for baking a stone into his loaf of bread
he finds his parents alive on the Lapland border. He
works as a fisherman for his father but wrecks both

117

boat and seine. He's accident-prone and can't get the knack of things:

> *Since he had been nurtured badly,*
> *Cradled wrongly as a child*
> *By the wicked foster-parent.*

Kullervo's story so far is told in Runes 31 to 34 of the *Kalevala*. You summarize their events orchestrally in the first two movements of the Symphony, but focus on Runes 35 and 36, 'Incest' and 'The Death of Kullervo', bringing in your male choir as narrator and the baritone and soprano voices of Kullervo and his sister for dramatic realism.

Kullervo's father sends him to pay the land taxes. On his way home he unknowingly ravishes his own sister who throws herself in the river when she realises she's committed incest (Third Movement). Rather than kill himself, Kullervo goes to war against his wicked uncle's tribe, 'the host of Unto', a very bad bunch. He wipes out his enemies, avenging his parents and his own ill-treatment as a child (Fourth Movement). Returning from the battle he comes to the place where he had deflowered his sister. Overcome with remorse he throws himself on the point of his sword (Fifth Movement). So, Sibelius, the applause that made you an overnight celebrity was for a dark, fateful story. What were you really saying? What can we learn about you from this doomed, heroic youth?

We'll join you in Vienna, 1891. You're studying orchestration and learning about the Austro-German musical tradition from Karl Goldmark and Robert Fuchs. A performance of Bruckner's Third Symphony convinces you that he is 'the greatest of all living composers'. Hans Richter conducts Beethoven's Ninth.

'You know', you write to Martin Wegelius, your composition teacher at the Helsinki Music Institute, 'I was so overwhelmed by it that I wept. I felt so small'.

118

You immerse yourself in the *Kalevala* and you're in love with Aino, daughter of the aristocratic Lieutenant-General Alexander Järnefelt, a prominent supporter of the Finnish language. From this crucible of influences comes the ambition to compose a Finnish work on a nineteenth-century Austro-German scale. It will speak of Finnish history through the mythic figures of the *Kalevala* and it will speak of love. Then you'll stop feeling small.

If Uncle Untamo's malice and the treachery of Ilmarinen's wife evoke Finland's subjugation by Sweden and Russia, Kullervo himself is you, Sibelius, thinly disguised. Like you, when your father died, he loses the security of his home. Like you, at least in your imagination, he is a solitary figure trying to make his way in a hostile world. Your secret engagement to Aino becomes the illicit seduction of a sister. Tabooed as practice, incest was acceptable as an expressive device, witness nature's blessing the love of Siegmund and Sieglinde in the '*Winterstürme wichen dem Wonnemond*' passage in Act I of *Die Walküre*. Surely the coming together of Kullervo and his sister is your message to Aino about the intense, blood-kinship kind of affinity you feel for her. You love her so much you'd fall on your sword to prove it. In November you'd felt the impact of a production of *Tristan und Isolde*. The implication of Kullervo's sister's suicide followed by his own is both remorse and *Liebestod*. It could all be reduced to three simple propositions: your love of Finland; your love for Aino; and, given your admiration for Bruckner's Third Symphony and Beethoven's Ninth, your determination to proclaim your allegiances in a work of essentially Finnish character on the grand European scale. So you did. Culturally you split the atom.

***

The programme note called *Kullervo* 'a symphonic poem', but in letters to Aino you referred to it as a symphony and did so even late in life. It's often alleged that after five performances you repudiated the work and withdrew it for ever. You judged it immature and were worried that people would deride its Finnishness, but we know that the fourth movement was played at a patriotic concert in 1905 and again, fifty years later, at a concert for your 90th birthday. You never authorized publication, but you never quite let go of *Kullervo*. How could you? Its success persuaded Aino's father to let you marry 'the prettiest girl in Finland'; it had made you a hero of Finnish culture; and it led to a commission from the conductor, Robert Kajanus, to compose the symphonic poem *En Saga*. This encouraged you to focus on orchestral expression. But what forms should you choose to express yourself in?

After the first performance of Brahms's Fourth Symphony in 1885 the German critic, Friedrich von Hausegger defined the musical match of the day.

'The symphony is the key form around which the battle rages in our time', he said, 'It is in the symphony that the composer of today reveals himself, and by so doing commits himself one way or the other'.

The battle in question was between the party of Liszt and Wagner and the Viennese classical tradition. Lisztians and Wagnerites were all for the programme symphony, music drama and an assault on tonality; the traditionalists supported the legacy of Beethoven, tonality and the sanctity of form. Debussy thought the symphony moribund; Strauss chose music drama and the symphonic poem. Which party would get your vote?

120

You cast a double vote. When you tried your hand at music drama you got stuck with mediocre librettists. The *Building of the Boat,* about the young Väinämöinen's love for the daughter of the moon, refused to jell for want of dramatic energy. The potential for tableaux was there, but there wasn't enough action in the text to energize your musical imagination towards operatic expression. You couldn't make up your mind how much of a Wagnerite you were so it was hard to find an idiom; but its intended prelude gave you the draft for *The Swan of Tuonela.* Much of *The Maiden in the Tower* is musically below your best invention, the text is lame and the melodramatic story downright silly, on the level of pantomime, but it's a shame that the good bits aren't better known. A junky attends to everything you composed, always on the look-out for something to feed his habit, and wants to say to a friend, 'Listen to this. You've never heard it before. Isn't it like him? Isn't it good?' A junky wishes you'd salvaged the best music for a 'Maiden in the Tower' suite, using the sprightly overture, the first interlude between the first two scenes and especially the second between the third and fourth – a delicious Sibelian miniature – as well as the Maiden's prayer to Santa Maria and the Chorus's song to coming Spring in Scene 3, which so poignantly mocks the Maiden's wrongly presumed surrender of her purity. A junky doesn't want any of the good notes going to waste.

No, Sibelius, you weren't destined for opera. Nevertheless, *Kullervo,* your incidental music for the theatre and symphonic poems from *En Saga* to *Tapiola* allied you with the Liszt-Wagner faction. At the same time your seven purely orchestral post-*Kullervo* symphonies established your position in the 'classical' tradition.

121

By the time you came to write the work we know as Symphony No. 1 in E minor you were thirty-three, ten years younger than Brahms when his First Symphony was ready for performance. You'd prepared carefully, developing your palette in the *Karelia* music and the *Four Legends from the Kale*vala. Your gift as a miniaturist – on a par with Elgar's – was evident in the 'Musette' and 'Nocturne' of the music for Adolf Paul's play, *King* Christian II, anticipating the charming 'Pastorale' in *Pelléas et Mélisande*, the oriental procession at the beginning of *Belshazzar's Feast*, depictions of Swanwhite and the Prince in the music for Strindberg's play, *Swanwhite*, the sweetly melancholy *Andantino* from Act II of *Scaramouche*, Ariel's first song and Miranda's theme in *The Tempest*. On 26 April 1899, when you conducted the Symphony's first performance, each movement was applauded, if not as wildly as your choral *Song of the Athenians*. The Symphony was a triumph for Finnish art, but the *Song* brought the house down as a chorus of protest from the heart of Finnish nationalism (you!) against Tsar Nicholas II's clamp-down on Finland's nominally autonomous constitutional rights as a Grand Duchy under the brutish régime of the infamous Governor General Bobrikov.

> *Rise with thy strong arm furious, rise to fight*
> *for thy country,*
> *Hasten to yield up thy life, life for the races to*
> *come.*
> *Forward, striplings! Advance in columns*
> *inflexible, compact!*
> *Never the shadow of fear, never the panic of*
> *flight.*

What strength of creative will it must have taken to risk engagement with symphonic tradition.

Brahms could have told you how it felt to compose a symphony after Beethoven.

'You don't know what it's like', he wrote, 'to hear that giant marching along behind you'.

Brahms himself was marching behind you as well as Beethoven, Bruckner and all the rest, but the Finnish critic, Richard Faltin, praised the First Symphony's blend of personal and universal languages.

'The symphonic form placed no shackles on Sibelius's imagination...the composer speaks the language of all mankind, yet a tongue that is none the less his own'.

Its four-movement structure declares your allegiance to traditional form. The slow clarinet melody at the start of the first movement and its recurrence at the beginning of the finale recall Tchaikovsky who would have recognized his likeness in the lush *cantabile* theme of the finale. There's reminiscence of Bruckner in the scherzo and trio, but none of this detracts from the individuality of your musical energy and developing palette. We're in mature Sibelian hands in the first movement when a power surge of strings energizes the melodic line of the meditating clarinet. So you show thought and action working together, a unified dynamic. The over-all experience of the symphony is of a compellingly original imagination combining passionate intensity with a rage for order in an idiom already distinctively your own.

'I have never listened to any music that took me away so completely from our usual Western life, and transported me into a quite new civilization', wrote the eminent British music critic, Ernest Newman, 'Every page breathes of another manner of thought, another way of living, even another landscape and seascape than ours'.

Ian Whyte was leaning forward from his pillows, his back arched in the conducting crouch. His arms were outstretched, but not towards his orchestra in readiness for the first downbeat of a new performance. Patricia Henderson was standing in the open door of his room.

'Darling', he said as she went to him. The word was placed on the air with tonal precision not as a greeting or anything intended especially for her, but as a fact about the woman whose arms now held him in an image of tenderness in action.

I walked back down the path to the bus stop with the sway of the *andante* of the First Symphony requieming in my mind. I thought of the marvellous boy with the *Messiah* in his head, not quite stretching precocious legs to the organ pedals in Dalmeny Kirk, and of the conductor who went home from work with the telegram of your thanks for his wartime performance of the Second, and who cared what a boy at the back of the studio was listening to.

It was still drizzling, so I could lose my tears in the spatter of raindrops on my glasses. He died three months later. His son said, 'The rivers stood stock still and the birds froze in the trees'.

5. 'Duke of Argyll' and a son in music

After the war Scotland lolled in complacent paranoia. Since 1707 Scottish sensibility had either touched its forelock to England's supremacy in a nominal Britain, or whined about forces which had sabotaged an ancient nation. But there was no political will to self-determination like Finland's in 1917 when your people broke free from Russia or like southern Ireland's when the Irish cast off the British crown. As late as 1992 the writer Jan Morris was astonished by Scotland's political status, marvelling 'at the aberration of history that allows the kind of people who live up here to be governed, generation after generation, by the kind of people who live down there'. It was as if people fatalistically believed any hopeful attempt at social improvement would only make things worse.

Suppressed into the British role in Allied opposition to Nazi, Italian and Japanese fascisms, Scottish national consciousness gradually realized that if the northern part of the United Kingdom had helped to win the victory it had also lost, for the second time in thirty years, an unjust portion of the lion's share of the peace. The Festival of Britain on London's South Bank and the coronation of Queen Elizabeth in June 1953 proclaimed British determination to overcome post-war austerities, but for people like us such junketings seemed insensitively remote from a dour world of recent ration books and unconvincing socialism.

The Scottish North Briton was peripheral and perceived as an amalgam of clichés, some of which you'll probably recognize, Sibelius, they're so well known. The Scot was tight-fisted, brutish, maudlin, canny, repressed, volatile, grimly religious, a barbarian

125

colourful enough to be worth exhibiting as one of the world's ethnic sideshows. Mary Queen of Scots, Bonnie Prince Charlie, shortbread, oatcakes and whisky, unintelligible accents, the bonnie banks of Loch Lomond, the Massacre of Glencoe and the pibrochs the writer James Kennaway describes as 'damp, penetrating and sad like a mist' made a culture of kitsch assiduously fostered and marketed by a hungry tourist industry. The weather, as the great Canadian humourist Stephen Leacock knew, was infamous:

> *It was a gloriously beautiful Scotch morning.*
> *The rain fell softly and quietly, bringing*
> *dampness and moisture, and almost a*
> *sense of wetness to the soft moss underfoot.*
> *Grey mists flew hither and thither, carrying*
> *with them an invigorating rawness that*
> *had almost a feeling of dampness.*

Clichés beget ignorance: the visitors came and asked their questions.

'Excuse me', said one visitor to John Knox's house in Edinburgh's Royal Mile, 'but where did Knox keep the bodies he bought from Burke and Hare?' (The wrong man, sir, that was Dr Robert Knox, to whom in the late 1820s the murderers Burke and Hare sold cadavers for medical study, a pithy monomaniac assured of his gruesome immortality by James Bridie's portrait of him in the 1930 play, *The Anatomist*.)

Talking of *Treasure Island* a tourist guide remarked that Robert Louis Stevenson was sickly as a boy. 'My goodness', gushed a wide-eyed English lady, 'to think that he grew up and invented the railway engine'.

At Abbotsford, home of Sir Walter Scott, an American visitor wanted to see the cloak the chivalrous knight spread out for Queen Elizabeth; another remarked that 'Abbotsford sure was a big house for a ploughman'.

A third, doubtless wishing to highlight the ignorance of the others, chipped in with: 'Did Scott really write all these books before he went to the South Pole?'

On a higher plane of error Matthew Arnold commends Robert Burns for a view of the world that is 'large, free, shrewd, benignant – truly poetic, therefore', but finds that the poet, like Chaucer, falls short of the high seriousness of the great classics. This wouldn't be surprising in a poetry which, Arnold declares, deals 'perpetually with Scotch drink, Scotch religion and Scotch manners'. (Had he skipped the love poems or is love reducible to 'manners'? Was he deaf to song or just envious of Burns's appetite for a good time?) The drink needs no identifying, the manners derive from it and the religion is all too often either bigoted Protestant, bigoted Papist or, in the West of Scotland, the transposition of these into the blue and the green, Rangers and Celtic soccer teams, endemically clashing armies of an eternal cultural night. Jacobites notwithstanding, Calvin, certainly, has been more formative than the Holy See in post-Reformation Scotland, particularly since the Disruption of 1843 when some 40 per cent of the church establishment broke from the 'Auld Kirk' to form the ineptly named 'Free Church'. In the name of true Presbyterian values, the Free Church invested the good life with a gloom even Calvin and Sabbath-conscious John Mitchell would have found oppressive. Charles, Lord Neaves satirizes the consequences in what he calls 'A Lyric for Saturday Night':

We zealots made up of stiff clay,
  The sour-looking children of sorrow,
While not over-jolly today,
  Resolve to be wretched tomorrow.

We can't for a certainty tell
  What mirth may molest us on Monday;
But, at least, to begin the week well,
  Let us all be unhappy on Sunday.

Abroad we forbid folks to roam,
  For fear they get social or frisky;
But of course they can sit still at home,
  And get dismally drunk upon whisky.

Arnold's assessment of Burns gives the impression of a mind programmed by the hackneyed triad – drink, religion and proletarian manners – before its engagement with the poetry: he found what he expected to find. The tartan-quilted gift-shop editions of Burns have perpetuated the sentimental cliché of the heaven-taught but wayward ploughman, a sexual athlete with a record-breaking capacity for 'whisky gill or penny wheep'. To make matters worse, the impression of a national proclivity to drink, uncouth manners and religion could be reinforced by modern instances.

'Butcher Boiled His Friend' proclaimed the front page of the Glasgow *Evening Times* on Wednesday 28th May 1980 in two-inch-high headlines. On the Glasgow subway a passenger showed his paper to the man sitting next to him.

'Hey, pal', he said, the brightness of hope in his eyes, 'see this? Good innit? Mibbee we've goat wurr ain Sweeney Todd efter a' these years'.

The butcher and his friend had been sharing a Friday-evening pint. An argument led to the exchange of insults, then of blows. A pickaxe was introduced and the friend lay dead. The butcher put the folded body of his friend in the shop's boiler, went home for his 'tea' and returned to the scene of the crime intending to mince the remains. When

EVENING Times

SCOTLAND'S GREATEST EVENING PAPER

No. 32,696 Wednesday, May 28, 1980 10p

BUTCHER BOILED HIS FRIEND

FATHER-OF-FOUR David Young today admitted boiling his friend in a vat of water after murdering him with a pickaxe.

And the 40-year-old Lanarkshire butcher was sent to the High Court for sentence.

The story of the macabre murder unfolded today at Hamilton Sheriff Court, where Young, of 29 Mavisbank Gardens, Bellshill, faced the murder charge.

By DAVID STEELE

the body through a mincer.

But the machine was too small—and Young then planned to take the

129

The Bellshill butcher

the mincer proved too small he planned to take the body to his mother's house which was empty as she was on holiday. Remorse struck early on Sunday. He confessed to his employer who called the police.

The *Times* reporter invited the butcher's tearful wife to comment. The accuracy of his quotation is a little suspect.

'I can't understand how he came to kill Andy Kerr with whom he was very friendly'.

Quintessentially Scottish according to Matthew Arnold. The story begins with drink, descends to violence and dissipates in Sabbath remorse, ending with the implausibly correct grammatical manners of the wife's 'with whom'.

There's an antidote waiting in a Glasgow pub, courtesy of you, Sibelius. Let's go there for a drink. We'll call the pub 'Duke of Argyll'. You'll notice that clientele is working class and drinking methodical. Lounge-bar niceties are spurned here; ladies are not banned as they were in the old days, but there are no wilting crisps, no soggy pickled onions. Men stand at the bar or sit at forthright tables, getting on with it. The pint glasses of 'Heavy' go up and down like the pistons of a Caledonian MacBrayne ferry plugging up the Sound of Mull.

'A right cauld yin the day', a man says, taking froth from his mouth with the back of his hand. It's not a complaint, not now that beer fades the day's memory of nipping winds on the building site. It's just a truth.

'Aye, right enough', a voice says, amiable, contented. A man settling to his evening.

Many are lit, some oiled, but order prevails. The bartender is a burly man with eyebrows like Highland cattle. His hands move, deft as a gunfighter's, from counter to sink to beer-tap to counter to till. His blue eyes attend; his customers know the score.

130

A Colossus comes in and orders a whisky – 'a wee goldie' – and a pint. He wears brown dungarees, a cloth cap pushed back on his head, heavy boots. Twenty minutes later, outside three whiskies and three pints, he begins to whistle, beating time to himself with his fingers on the counter. The man next to him at the bar turns his head.

'Heh Jimmy, whit's that yer whistlin'?'

Colossus doesn't seem to hear. He goes on with his whistling, fingers drumming, eyes fixed on the mirror behind the bar as if it reflects the grandeur he sees inside his head.

'Come on, Jimmy', the other man says, 'gie's the name o' yer tune'.

The whistling stops. The hand pauses in its drumming and a finger is pointed at the interlocutor.

'D'ye no' recognize it, ma friend?'

'Nuh. Ah doan reckernize it. 's nice, but ah doan reckernize it'.

'It's Sibelius, ma friend, Si-be-li-us', says Colossus, pronouncing the name as four majestic chords. 'Sibelius, Symphony Nummer Twa. That's the last bit o' it, *allegro moderato*'.

'Is that right?' says the other, vaguely impressed.

'Si-be-li-us', says Colossus. 'Magic. Sibelius is pure fuckin' magic'.

***

Sibelius, you might ask why a Glasgow artisan couldn't find his magic closer to home in a Scottish composer. What about the prolific Alexander Campbell Mackenzie, John Blackwood McEwen and Hamish McCunn? Part of the answer is that by the 1950s they'd virtually disappeared. Ian Whyte's music had

131

died with him except for occasional performances of the concert overture, *Edinburgh*, Scotland's answer to Elgar's *Cockaigne*. Mackenzie was remembered not for his five operas but for his long reign as Principal of London's Royal College of Music and his 'notable gift of frenzy'. McEwen's *Solway Symphony* and *Three Border Ballads* were forgotten until the CD revolution demanded new repertoire and brought them back into the recording studio if not to the concert hall. Hamish McCunn's opera, *Jeanie Deans*, based on Sir Walter Scott's novel, *The Heart of Midlothian*, was performed in England in the 1890s, but by the time our Glaswegian Colossus was setting up his whiskies and pints in the 'Duke of Argyll' only his attractive but light-weight romantic concert overture, *The Land of the Mountain and the Flood*, composed when he was nineteen, could be heard on Scottish radios. In any case, none of this music could compete with the Second Symphony which was broadcast often.

Two English composers were nourished by Scotland, Sir Granville Bantock, and Sir Arnold Bax. First heard at a concert in Glasgow in 1916, your friend Bantock's *Hebridean Symphony* uses themes derived from Scottish folk music, including the Highland pipe tune, the 'Pibroch of Donnail Dhu' and the 'Harris Love-lament'. Bantock's *Celtic Symphony* also makes use of Hebridean folksong, in particular 'Sea-longing'.

> *Sore sea-longing in my heart*
> *Blue deep Barra waves are calling.*

As Scottish in feeling as Max Bruch's popular *Scottish Fantasy*, and more original, the *Celtic Symphony* is scored for string orchestra and, hang the expense, six harps which, of course, puts live performance beyond most concert budgets.

133

Glencolumcille, West Donegal

Now let's listen to the chords of a single harp ripple through a passionate song for strings. Where does this haunting music come from? There are hints of Ravel but the music is English in origin. It's not English in character. It's a Harp Quintet and the harp is the clue to something Celtic. It might be a *clarseach*, an indigenously Irish or Scottish harp requisitioned by a strikingly independent musical imagination, classically schooled but romantically inclined. A dreamer, Sibelius, like you.

In the West Donegal seaside village of Glencolumcille, outside a whitewashed cottage tweed shop, an old weaver sits on a bench in the watery Irish sun. We join him.

'Can you tell us anything about an English composer who often came here in the early 1900s?'

'Sir Arnold Bax, Master of the King's Musick', comes the reply, quick as you like.

'Do you remember the other name he was known by in Ireland?'

'Dermot O'Byrne, story-teller and poet'.

We buy a length of the speckled cloth by way of thanks for the conversation. The old man has closed time's gap and put us there with Arnold Bax the musician, otherwise known as the writer, Dermot O'Byrne, in his juicy, impressionable twenties, pondering the restless chiarascuros of the north Atlantic, the mythologizing fantasies of Irish folk-tales and, most of all, the poetry of Yeats. 'I came upon W. B. Yeats's "The Wanderings of Oisin" in 1902', Bax says in his memoir, *Farewell My Youth*, 'and in a moment the Celt within me stood revealed'.

Yeats's Oisin and Donegal's Glencolumcille were a long way from the upper-crust English life of servants and private schooling Bax was born into on 8th November 1883. Substantial unearned incomes

Near Glencolumcille, West Donegal

enabled Arnold to follow his musical bent untroubled by other employment and his brother Clifford to devote his life to literature. At Ivybank, their mild-mannered father's mansion in London's then rural Hampstead, life was crisply administered by their much younger, strong-willed but warm-hearted mother. The brothers read voraciously, played exuberant cricket and left home as soon as they could. After five years at the Royal Academy of Music Arnold travelled to Dresden for the city's fleshpots, big helpings of Wagner, an early performance of Strauss's *Salome*, and his introduction to Mahler whose work, rather like you, Sibelius, he found 'eccentric, long-winded, muddle-headed, and yet always interesting'.

With the Easter Rising in 1916 his dream-lit Ireland was dead and gone. He had already lived a crammed, storm-tossed life. Infatuated with the volatile pianist, Harriet Cohen, he had proclaimed his ardour in the Freudian waves that smash into the castle-crowned cliff of *Tintagel*, the best known of his tone poems. Even with her as champion and vehicle of his music, his known world was, in Yeats's words, 'All changed, changed utterly'. The War's death toll included many friends. He was cushioned by financial security, but looked back and pined for what was not, looked forward and fretfully wondered. It was time to push beyond the pageantry of the tone poems described by brother Clifford as 'adolescent dreams of more than life can give'. How should he begin? He was a master of the orchestra and, like you, a devotee of form. The obvious answer was the symphony. So a new journey of exploration and enquiry began in 1921 with the First Symphony and ended in 1939 with the Seventh. There was darkness behind, was more darkness still to come?

The emotional setting of Bax's seven symphonies is grim in the spirit of Matthew Arnold's 'Dover Beach' where life is a 'darkling plain' of 'confused alarms' and

137

Morar, Inverness-shire

'ignorant armies' clashing by night. The symphonies make up an idiosyncratic but universalizing narrative of questions, crises and hard-earned moments of repose. The emotion is always frontal, demanding attention. Nice work, if we can get it, but we can only get it if we sit down and listen through saturated textures – Bax's intricacies can be forbidding – to the detailed elisions and thematic metamorphoses within. The true appeal of these symphonies is to the listener disposed to hear concentrated musical speech about primal human things, the 'foul rag and bone shop' of a composer's heart. So they belong to the same world as yours, Sibelius, and to the Russian party of Tchaikovsky and Shostakovich rather than the British party of Elgar, Holst and Vaughan Williams. He dedicated his Fifth Symphony to you and according to Harriet Cohen you called him 'my son in music'. The Englishman who felt himself a Celt was an honorary Finn by adoption.

It's often said that Bax's music reveals affinities with the natural forces of his environment. This is hardly surprising when he so carefully chose environments which would accommodate his self-consciously romantic character. He found Ireland first, then its counterpart in Scotland. They were his Karelia. The village of Morar sits in its stone houses on a ridge in Invernesshire above silver sands. The young Bax had sampled the coasts of north-western Scotland and found in them echoes of his beloved Irish landscapes. So in the autumn of 1928, in the youth of middle age at 45, he packed the sketches for his Third Symphony and took the train from London to connect with the West Highland Line, bound for Morar. In summer the place is a tourist's photogenic dream: the sands flash white across the Sound of Sleat to the isles of Eigg, Rum and Skye. But Bax went there at the end

139

Bax's view of Rum from Morar

of the year, when the sands would be pock-marked by rain, episodically visible in the mist or coldly lit by the short flare of a northern sun. In Room 11 of the Station Hotel he sat in polar conditions, wearing a heavy winter coat, looking across another ebony sea to the purple isles while he orchestrated his most frequently performed symphony.

The Third Symphony is probably his most Sibelian symphony, and a crucial stage in his development of symphonic form. He had settled on a structure of three movements for the first two symphonies, but had ended both with passages that pulled out from the argument of their last movements into summations or reflective backward looks. In the Third this concluding passage is extended into the first of his symphonic Epilogues. After the broodings and upheavals of its first movement, the sea-music of the slow movement brings detachment without resolution, a Sibelian sense of emotion observed. The third movement hammers out a hard new question and tries to answer it with a dance of forced optimism. We are impressed by the effort, wish we could be convinced. The music subsides. What next? The Epilogue brings its answer in the simplicity of a floating melody on oboes and clarinets over the endorsing pulse of a softly swinging rhythm and Bax's symphonic fable ends in other-worldly delicacies of harp, horn and solo violin. If we're to be fully human we are doomed to probe the mysteries of brutality and beauty in the world and in ourselves. We must exercise our wills in the quest for what Herman Melville calls 'the ungraspable phantom of life'. We won't grasp the phantom, of course, but if we're true to the quest, grace and repose may come at last from beyond the scope of human will, perhaps mystically from nature, like this.

Right enough, Big Man, this is your 'son in music' talking.

141

Isles of Eigg and Rum from Morar

***

In 1988 spectacular fireworks would open Glasgow's Garden Festival, a wasteland site on the Clyde transformed into a park with flowers of every colour, variety and arrangement. The five-month-long festival was the largest public event held in Scotland since the Empire exhibition of 1938. In 1990 Jacques Chirac would anoint the city Cultural Capital of Europe and in 1999 Glasgow would beat Liverpool and Edinburgh for the title of European City of Architecture and Design. Epidemics of stone-blasting and planting would make it cleaner and greener, resurrecting Daniel Defoe's vision of 'the cleanest and beautifullest, and best built city in Britain, London excepted'. Sports and arts centres, delicatessens and wine bars would magnetize an expanding population of Yuppies and new technologies would prosper where forges and shipyards had died. An urban phoenix.

But nobody knew that yet. It was a dreich city in the fifties and early sixties, peevish and down in the mouth like the old jingle about the symbolism of its arms:

> *This is the tree that never grew,*
> *This is the bird that never flew,*
> *This is the fish that never swam,*
> *This is bell that never rang.*

Neither the 'Duke of Argyll' nor occasional top-ups of Lismore could erase memories of the fog years, war and fear of the future. I wanted away from falling and rising damp and ossified class antagonisms. Enough of kitsch nationalism and girning politicians. Enough of what the great Renaissance scholar, George Buchanan, called 'English lies and Scottish

142

vanity'. I wanted new styles of landscape, sun, colour, effervescence. Maybe the elusive fun was somewhere out there. So, Sibelius, we went to Africa, joined the crusade against *apartheid* and fell in love with Margaret.

6. Kwela

The dawn of a new political day for South Africa seemed achingly remote in the 1970s when Johnny Clegg and Sipho Mchunu broke through the colour line to create the popular group, Juluka.

African sky blue, your children wait for the dawn
African sky blue, soon a new day will be born,
African sky blue, African sky blue,
Will you bless my life?

Their song of protest was daringly explicit compared to the indirectness of your *Finlandia* against Russianisation. If they'd tried that sort of thing in Moscow they'd have had a midnight call from the KGB descendants of Ivan the Terrible's *oprichniki*. Even Shostakovich had his bag of necessaries packed in case of a knock on the door and a one-way ride to the gulag archipelago. The Stasi would have been on to them in the German Democratic Republic. In the 1980s, when the *apartheid* régime was fighting opposition with dirty tricks and death squads, Clegg and Mchunu might have vanished into the cesspool of state-sponsored crimes against dissidents.

When would South Africa bless the lives of non-whites with social justice? Only after the death of *apartheid* would the African sun warm the eyes of its black children and the rivers dance for the millions relegated to second, third or sub-class citizenship in the land of their forefathers. Racial domination is a feature of colonial enterprises but in South Africa as *apartheid* it was uniquely refined and systematized.

'*Apartheid* is as evil and vicious as Nazism and Communism; the Government will fail completely for it is ranging itself on the side of evil, injustice and oppression'.

145

So said Bishop Desmond Tutu, awarded the 1984 Nobel Peace Prize for his leadership in the battle against *apartheid*. The idea of segregation by race wasn't invented by South African nationalists and it wasn't a conventional political system, so it yielded little to conventional political pressure. Drawing strength from a religious faith, deeply held by the Afrikaner, it began when the first white man set foot on the continent. The earliest law against inter-marriage between 'Europeans and slaves of full colour' was enacted in 1682; the first Pass Laws in 1809. The designation of separate areas for blacks and whites dates from 1829.

'It has now become an accepted axiom in our dealings with the natives that it is dishonourable to mix white and black blood', declared the revered Jan Smuts, in London in 1917. This was a lauded South African leader, a good guy, on our side in World War II, with a much-vaunted intellect and world-wide influence.

When the Nationalist Party came to power in 1948 they legislated for a way of life that had been followed for 300 years. In so doing they brought the world's attention to an iniquitous state of affairs which, until then, the British had helped to develop and the world had condoned. Ten years later the election of Dr H. F. Verwoerd as Prime Minister inaugurated the granite age of *apartheid*. He opposed any kind of racial mixing, not only miscegenation, but any kind of contact whether physical, social or even the casual contacts of pedestrians in the streets.

'Europeans and non-Europeans scattered and mixed up about the whole of South Africa', he said, giving full rein to his repugnance in a speech to the Senate, 'Europeans and non-Europeans travelling mixed up in the trams and the trains; Europeans

146

and non-Europeans are already mixing in hotels and places where meals are served; non-Europeans engaged more and more in taking possession of the theatres and the streets; engaged in seeking learning which they do not use in the service of their own people, but which they use in order to cross the borderline of European life, to become traitors to their own people'.

In 1959 Ezekiel Mphahlele clarified the attitude of an educated black towards the white man in his autobiography, *Down Second Avenue*:

> *He has driven me against the wall so that I*
> *never forget I am black. He has taught me to*
> *lie to him and feel triumphant. Because he has*
> *made me get used to the back door I have bought*
> *goods, stolen from his shop by his own Black*
> *worker, for less than the cost. And there are*
> *millions of me. We know almost everything about*
> *him and he knows nothing about us, so we still*
> *hold the trump card.*

What can élitist classical music music do against this kind of sickness, Sibelius? Juluka drummed, plucked, piped and chanted its populist defiance of Verwoerd's supremacist obscenity. Clegg, a white bi-cultural social anthropologist and Mchunu, a Zulu gardener from Johannesburg, sang of the new warfare required by the continuing struggle:

> *The warrior's now a worker*
> *And his war is underground,*
> *With cordite in the darkness*
> *He milks the bleeding veins of gold,*
> *When the smoking rock-face murmurs*
> *He always thinks of you,*
> *African sky blue,*
> *Will you see him through?*

'What can I know? What can I dream? What can I hope? What will the future bring?' Juluka were still asking in the '70s and '80s. In 1965 when I left South Africa hope seemed absurd and the future bloody.

Without knocking the graduate student entered my office softly, nodded, finger to lips, and went to my bookcase. He slid the books out shelf by shelf, checking for bugs. Then behind the pictures. He came round to my side of the desk to bend and look and feel underneath.

'Sorry', he said, exhaling, 'but you know how it is. They're everywhere'.

He sat, across the desk from me, breathed heavily, wiped sweat from his face.

'We know you're on the right side', he said, 'I've come to ask if you'll help us'.

'How?'

I might receive a phone call. Perhaps I'd be told to meet someone, accept a package, take it home, no questions asked. Later there could be another phone call instructing me to deliver the package somewhere. There might be explosions. Would I be willing to follow such instructions? We both knew the system was evil, had to be cut down.

'Please'.

'Give me until tomorrow'..

No sleep that night. Knowing I'd decline the gambit I dreaded meeting my student in the morning to expose my lack of moral fibre. But there was no meeting. The Special Branch had raided Liliesleaf farm in the northern Johannesburg suburb of Rivonia, headquarters of *Umkhonto we Sizwe, 'The Spear of the Nation',* military arm of the African National Congress. Mandela and his comrades were in custody, expecting the death sentence. My student had fled to Swaziland.

148

Incapable of working with cordite in the darkness, I knew I wasn't the kind of political activist required by the intensifying struggle. I lacked the nerves for a career as academic Pimpernel. I had a child to consider. Or was it simply that I didn't have the guts? What would you have done, Sibelius? Would you have taken such instruction, or joined forces with Clegg and Mchunu? If you'd been a South African, or just there, like me, would you have recognized a moral obligation to come down from symphonic heights and co-opt your abstracting genius into the struggle? Would you have convened strings, brass, woodwind, timpani in a symphonic act of protest against the concerted racist malice of a culture? Would you have believed that the poison of apartheid called on you to make music of defiance and affirmation? Would you have heard the child's prayer, black this time? Could you have cured the apartheid disease in the kingdom of the big tune, or would you have let it go as *Valse Triste*? Would it have been enough that your music helped some of us to keep the faith with a value system antithetical to the evil system?

***

When I was eleven I decided I would go to South Africa. Fascination with the country was instilled by an exhibition in Glasgow's MacLellan Galleries. Photographs of story-book animals, pictures and models of gold and diamond mines, images of African people as part of a happy, industrious, exotic human swarm were presented to my group of children-out-of-school by a brisk, bird-like woman with an oddly beguiling accent. The pictures emanated rhythm, purpose, light, even smell. The woman's voice clinched it. Her use of English told me that my own language

149

could be a key to this brilliantly lit, multi-coloured country, and her accent meant that the spoken word would be interestingly different from what I heard around me every day in Glasgow. It was clear that everything else would be even more interestingly different.

Sibelius, you were looking for the stimuli of difference as well as instruction and musical experience when you travelled to Berlin, Vienna, Rome and Rapallo. Similarly, in 1962, equipped with an MA and a head full of your music I was looking for difference. Eager to experience the vibrancies of a culture I pictured as remote from Presbyterian Scotland, naively unaware of the similarities between South African racism and the antisemitic psychosis of Nazi Germany, I went to work as a lecturer in English at Rhodes University in the Eastern Cape Province city of Grahamstown. When the anguish of apartheid made its impact I remembered Abraham Lincoln's conviction that 'there is a special place in hell for those who remain neutral in a moral crisis'. So, instead of leaving there and then, I joined the South African Liberal Party, inspired by the pre-eminent membership of Alan Paton who knew so well how the beloved country cried. This was the only political party which stood for universal franchise.

Literature is about values, so in the South African context it became a moral science of subversion. If I could have got away with it I'd have played the students your symphonies – there's nothing so subversive as music – but professionally I only had words to work with. The temptation was to apply everything to the political situation; after all, what use were mere aesthetics to the struggle? *Othello* was a gift: once you had revealed the quality of Iago's evil

Rhodes University, Grahamstown

you had exposed *apartheid*'s Immorality Act as devil's work. Conrad's *Nostromo* was another: the silver of his imaginary South American mine equalled the gold of the Rand and the contamination of Charles Gould's idealism by material interests illuminated the protectionism that kept *apartheid* going. Jo, the crossing-sweeper in Dickens's *Bleak House*, was re-born as little Alfred who always managed to be waiting with hand outstretched under an impish grin at the end of the day, although the police were for ever moving him on. Even Spenser was hi-jacked into relevance. What was the description of Lucifera in Book One of *The Faerie Queene* if not an allegory of Verwoerd's National Party:

> *rightfull kingdome she had none at all,*
> *Ne heritage of native soveraintie;*
> *But did usurpe with wrong and tyrannie*
> *Upon the scepter which she now did hold:*
> *Ne ruld her realm with lawes but pollicie,*
> *And strong advizement of six wisards old,*
> *That, with their counsels bad, her kingdome*
>   *did uphold.*

You got your students to read that and invited them to identify the six wickedest wizards in the Nationalist cabinet – even when you knew there was a Special Branch spy at the back of the class and the police were watching your house.

But Liberal affirmation and applied literature seemed increasingly paltry as the situation worsened. The Special Branch of the police took a friend in for questioning. He wasn't tortured: they just kept him standing for four days. That left no incriminating marks on his body, but altered his mind for ever. I knew it was time to go. As the *Cape Town Castle* headed out of Table Bay for

152

Southampton I realized that I already felt guilty for leaving. I'd only been in South Africa for three years but for some twenty years more I dreamed about the country. I never stopped loving it, but I never thought I would see it again.

Twenty-seven years later, in August 1992, an invitation to make a lecture tour of South African universities put me on a flight to Johannesburg. It was a surprise to find that South African Airways publicity – magazines and video material – still presented the multi-coloured country as a prosperous, sunlit playground for whites with a few happy darkies chorically in the background for ethnic cuteness. I would have expected a change in promotional images, even if only to modify the implications of the traditional élitist English/Afrikaans bilingualism. What would the new South Africa's official languages be – Zulu, Tswana, Xhosa?

My first breakfast was in the well-appointed dining room of a Johannesburg motel where well-dressed Africans, Indians and whites ate together. I thought of what it would have been like in the sixties and how bizarre it was that on this first day of an African National Congress strike, with breaking news of intimidation and burning tyres on railway lines, here were all the races breakfasting quietly together with morning radio playing jaunty African pop. Was *apartheid* only an evil dream? A friend from the past took me to his home. The house, like so many in Johannesburg, Durban, Cape Town and other cities, was surrounded by a high fence, topped by spikes. All windows and doors were stoutly barred. Despite such expensive measures to make fortresses of their houses, most people appeared to have been burgled at least once. Now the daily complexity of the new South Africa was making itself felt.

153

'Do not walk alone in Johannesburg' was the repeated warning.

Sibelius, let's listen to a white woman. She's just been to a champagne breakfast at a 300-year-old farm in the Cape. She's been invited to the breakfast with a group of other women by the then President's wife, Marike de Klerk. It's March 1993. The President's wife has been urging the women to become involved in the political process. She's been telling them about her plans for a foundation to assist women in rural areas.

'Was it a useful meeting?' we ask.

'The message was uplifting and positive', she replies. 'The informal conversation that took place around our table was not. Two years ago we would have talked about those things that make up a woman's world; career problems, childcare worries, men. Now we talked about guns. With the exception of myself, everyone present owned a firearm. We also exchanged tips: how to deal with the problem of stone-throwing when driving to Cape Town's D.F. Malan airport (stay in the fast lane, avoid the first turnoff); how to handle restaurant robberies (don't wear jewellery but do take cash so as not to irritate the muggers); how to foil car hijackers in Johannesburg (slow down when approaching a red light but never stop)'.

Only two years before the President's wife's uplifting breakfast the problems created by *apartheid* were not part of 'a woman's world'. Why, in 1991, weren't these women talking about the imminent historic changes which would irrevocably mingle their privileged, protected lives with the rainbow realities of their hitherto suppressed African, Indian and Coloured sisterhood? How would they rate their security anxieties against an African's humiliation

154

by the white man's city. The poet, Mongane Wally Serote, reports:

This way I salute you:
My hand pulses to my back trousers pocket
Or into my inner jacket pocket
For my pass, my life,
Jo'burg City.
My hand like a starved snake rears my
    pockets
For my thin, ever lean wallet,
While my stomach groans a friendly smile to
    hunger...
I can feel your roots, anchoring your might,
    my feebleness
In my flesh, in my mind, in my blood,
And everything about you says it,
That, that is all you need of me.

So walking in Johannesburg wasn't good for him either. For most of his life in the old South Africa he'd been in a much worse position than a white lady in the cocoon of her car, driving nervously to Cape Town's airport in the almost new South Africa. She might complain. He wasn't going to forget.

***

In a music store I found a CD of the original-cast recording of the 1959 musical *King Kong* and a disc by the legendary Spokes Mashiyane, 'King of *Kwela*'. *King Kong* was in its time a model of the anti-*apartheid* artistic co-operation later achieved by Juluka and other groups. Production, script and direction were by whites, but the show used black singers – including Miriam Makeba – actors and musicians and a musical conception by Todd Matshikiza to tell the tragic story of South African

155

Margaret and Charlotte

black heavyweight boxing champion Ezekial 'King Kong' Dhlamini. Opera, you might say, Sibelius, opera with its own home-grown aesthetics, but no *Don Giovanni* or *Rosenkavalier*; opera working for oppressed people in need of art about themselves.

The disc of *kwela* music was a CD re-mastering of an LP I had owned and loved in the sixties. Finding the music again put me into time-warp and back in touch with the complexities of the old South Africa, the resilience, intelligence, grace and vulnerability of African people, the venomous inhumanity of the system and the ineffectuality of attempts to make life good in a society which rejected decency as if it were an alien organ.

Margaret was the maid who kept the house clean and looked after Charlotte, my one-year-old daughter, during the day. She was Xhosa, in her late twenties. The master-servant relationship was repugnant both intrinsically and because it buttressed the caste system on which *apartheid* was based. But even politically liberal people, then as now, employed African servants because it was a way of getting domestic help while supporting them financially and knowing them well enough to be able to help with their food, medical needs, clothing and costs connected with the education of their children. Margaret was mentally and physically quick, with a ready and radiant smile. Like so many black South Africans she was fluent in three languages, English, Afrikaans and Xhosa. How cruelly ironic it was that African women, downgraded by *apartheid*, were judged capable of looking after white children and often, for their own survival, required to achieve linguistic proficiencies that would have been taken as signs of outstanding ability in a white student at school or university. Falling in love with her was easy.

She knew I'd joined Liberal Party. She knew I carried anti-*apartheid* placards at demonstrations in the town square. When I got home she helped me to wipe pro-*apartheid* spittle from my clothes. She knew we were on the same side.

Oh, Sibelius, how we needed the humanizing truth of your aspiring spirit in that time of injustice, brutality and fear. Remember Sweden's long grip of Finland; think of the Russian fist and your song of protest in *Finlandia*. Come into this memory. Dance with Margaret and all the dispossessed, dance to the *Freedom Charter* for South Africa, aching to cut loose from its chains.

> *South Africa belongs to all who live in it*
> *The people shall govern*
> *Peace and security for our children*
> *No more war*
> *Hamba Pietermaritzburg*
> *Every man and woman shall have a right to*
>   *vote*
> *For the people by the people with the people*
> *South Africa is our land no more war*

Margaret was curious about my choice of music. When she heard a record playing she'd stand by the living room door, cock her head to one side and listen intently, gradually developing a personal anthology of favourites. There was no predicting her taste. I don't think she'd ever been on a train, maybe she'd never seen one, but she adored Villa-Lobos's 'Little Train of the Caipira' from *Bachianas Brasileiras* No. 2, where the toccata-style runs and chords make an onomatopoeic sound picture of the train puffing, wheezing, rattling and tooting into heartland peasant country. She feigned terror and giggled at the *crescendi* in the *Allegretto* of Haydn's 'Military'

Symphony. There was nothing 'Macabre' for her about Saint-Saëns' ever popular 'Danse', just a good tune and a rhythm to agitate her broom over the polished wooden floors. 'The Sorcerer's Apprentice' was a similar hit, so I told her about Mickey Mouse and Leopold Stokowski in Disney's *Fantasia*. She thought Dvorak's 'Slavonic Dances' were like smiles, but the biggest laughs were the reluctant mule's hee-haw, violin cadenza and jogging cowboy tune in the 'On the Trail' movement of Ferde Grofé's *Grand Canyon Suite*.

In the dry heat of the African summer I often played your Sixth Symphony. 'Pure cold spring water', you called it. Margaret liked that idea and my stories about The Big Man. You thought other composers of the day were making 'highly spiced cocktails'.

'The older I grow', you said, 'the more classical I become'.

No doubt you were reacting against the exorbitant soul-searchings of Mahler and the sensualities of Richard Strauss, maybe taking a stand against the modernist astringencies of Stravinsky and Schoenberg. No doubt the pleasure I found in the coolness and clarity of the Sixth was a reaction against the hysterical impurities of *apartheid* as well as the summer's mind-bending heat and dust. It was my air-conditioner.

When you were planning the Symphony in 1918 you envisaged something less cool. The music would be 'wild and impassioned in character. Sombre pastoral contrasts. Probably in four movements with the end rising to a sombre roaring in the orchestra in which the main theme is drowned'. Five years later, when you conducted the first performance, it was evident that the act of composition had reversed the original plan to produce a work predominantly pastoral

159

with sombre contrasts. The serene polyphony of its beginning conjures pellucid northern air, Finnish firs in a gentle breeze, crystalline streams and the exhilarations of being contentedly out of doors. Nature sings in the pastoral tones of flutes and oboes, trips winsomely on skipping strings. Thunder rumbles but keeps its distance. Earth and music commune with each other in the second movement – voices may become a little raised in argument, but never shrill. The high-spirited third movement is more of a gallop than its nominal *poco vivace*. After antiphonal questions and answers between strings, woodwind and horns the last movement quickens – here comes the roaring. The forest god, Tapio, may be taking a break from his work of winter but he doesn't intend to be forgotten. At last a chorale-like figure assures us that for a moment, even in Africa, all is as clear and cool as it was at the Symphony's tranquil beginning.

Margaret learned to recognize the Sixth. She'd nod gravely, pointing to the record player.

'Ah, Master is listenin' to his water from The Big Man'.

Best of all she liked my record of Spokes Mashiyane's *kwela* music. ('*Kwela*' is a Zulu word meaning 'Climb up' or 'Get on top'.) I'm pretty sure you'd have liked it too, Sibelius, for its rhythm, sweetness and nostalgia. This music comes down from the time when Africans hollowed out short pieces of reed and made them into pipes for playing simple tunes. Spokes taught himself to play the traditional three-holed reed flute while tending his father's cattle in the Northern Transvaal. The metal descendant of the improvised reed instrument had become a 4/6d store-bought article by the time my record was made, Spokes was famous and, of course,

160

American jazz had arrived. Sometimes, before she began her housework for the day, Margaret would confront me with her megawatt smile.

'Master, play me Spokes, play me your *kwela!*'

I'd put the record on and she would go off to the room she was cleaning. When I passed the open door of the room I'd see her doing her dusting-dance, hips swaying, feet pointing the rhythm as she flicked the duster at pieces of furniture, her static partners.

When Margaret came to baby-sit in the evening I'd collect her from her house, although this was strictly illegal as I had no police pass to the African location where she lived, sharing a single cold-water tap with some twenty or more other families. Water queues were part of the daily routine. Here twenty children died every month from kwashiorkor, the viciously crippling disease caused by malnutrition. One night I went to fetch her as usual, turning from the tar-sealed highway into the pitted and ill-lit dirt road of the African location. Stopped outside her house I noticed that the flickering candlelight in the window of a house across the street had suddenly dimmed. Someone was looking out, watching and wondering why a white man had come. Such a visitor could be friendly, but I might be trouble, possibly Special Branch, even if I was driving a Volkswagen and not the tell-tale Studebaker 'Lark' favoured by the South African equivalent of the KGB. Margaret opened her door to my knock.

'Hello, Master, come in, Master'.

In the tiny living-room a man and woman were sitting on straight-backed wooden chairs. On a table in front of them a radio was playing African township music. It might have been the young Miriam Makeba and the Skylarks.

Margaret introduced me to her friends who were plainly embarrassed by the presence of a questionable

161

white man, and then withdrew to the other room of the house to finish her preparations for the evening. I sat at the table and there was an awkward mixture of strained conversation, shuffling feet and silence. I made a clumsy joke about revolutionizing South Africa by replacing Dr Verwoerd with Wilfred, a well-known petrol-pump attendant at a nearby garage. Uneasy laughter.

Now wearing her coiled head-dress and best red jersey, Margaret came back into the room at exactly the moment when the radio began to play *kwela* music. Margaret tensed, went into her smile, held out her hands towards the radio, then to me.

'Master, show them your *kwela*!'

I stood up and faced her. We began to dance. The man and woman laughed and began to clap. Then they pushed their chairs back, stood and danced too. We all danced to this sweet, sad, funny, wise music with its nonchalant vamping backgrounds to make you laugh and an ease that was pure and guileless to make you cry for valour and vulnerability. Because of *kwela* and the spirit of Margaret for a few minutes that night in the Cape Province in 1964 there was no *apartheid*.

'We are *umtya nethunga*', Margaret said. We were like the milk thong and the milk pail, as closely related as the thong for tying the cow's legs is to the pail for catching the milk

A few weeks later I was telephoned at my office by a woman who worked in the building next to my house.

'Come quickly', she said. 'Your little girl is playing in the street. There's a lot of traffic and I think your maid is drunk'.

I found Charlotte hopping off and on the edge of the pavement. Some drivers hooted as they passed,

162

but none was stopping to question the safety of a small child perilously close to a constant stream of cars and apparently unattended by her almost recumbent minder. Margaret was sitting on the grass verge, rocking, humming and talking to herself, her woollen hat angled over one eye. When I picked up my daughter and walked towards the house she followed unsteadily. In the kitchen I found the brandy bottle, nearly empty, and told Margaret she must leave at once. She walked out of the back door which I locked, went to the front of the house and tried unsuccessfully to climb back in through the windows, yelping like a hurt animal. For the next two weeks she knocked on my front door every morning.

'Master, take me back. This is my house with you, Master. I love you, Master. I come back'.

I gave her money and told her to go away. I was part of the system and needed a trustworthy baby-sitter. Margaret was gone; *apartheid* was back.

***

If Douglas the bully was Paul Robeson's revenge for the broken record of 'Ol' Man River', maybe Margaret's was the encephalitis that struck the day after I sent her away. Africa is full of magic, like your Karelia, Sibelius.

Cold watermelon couldn't coax the thermometer down from 104 degrees Fahrenheit but it gave the illusion of relief. I got up from my chair in the living room to take my plate through to the kitchen, missed the door and walked into the wall. Incredulity dulled consciousness of buckling knees, the fall, the uncoordinated attempts to stand on waxy limbs which ignored whatever messages the brain was trying to send them. Slowly I got up from the floor like a badly articulated marionette. My gyroscope was gone. A vice clamped my head and tightened fast. It seemed wise to reach a bed before my eyes were squeezed from their sockets.

It was late afternoon but there was far too much light. The room had more windows than usual. I realised I was hallucinating. Under the windows, facing into the room, the Queen's Eye Specialist in Scotland was working at his desk.

'In the meantime' he said without looking up, 'keep your eyes closed as much as possible'. He faded, before I could say anything, into the piercing light.

When I'd made it to the bed, I promised my eyes, I'd close them to keep them inside my head. My body was a bowling ball of incalculable bias. Aiming for two or three feet to the left of the door from the living room I set out across the tilting floor. On the fourth attempt I got through to the hallway, navigated my mutinous body into the bedroom by the same method, fell on the bed and shut my eyes.

'Margaret, I'm sorry', I said out loud, 'Forgive me. Please come back. I miss you. Let's forget it. I love you. We're *umtya nethunga*. Don't do this. I'm so sorry'.

The screw of the vice turned. How could I get to the bathroom cabinet for a pain-killer on legs that wouldn't obey orders? I opened my eyes. There was too much light in this room as well. I looked at the mantelpiece on the other side of the room. Its only ornament was a red and white porcelain horse like a three-dimensional illustration from a book of Russian folk tales. Abruptly, without so much as a whinny, it became two horses. The light was knives so I closed my eyes again but opened them when I realized I needed a doctor and commanded my body to begin the return trip to the telephone in the hall. I was alone in the house so I would need to call the doctor and unlock the front door for him to come in.

Samuel Beckett supplied the means of locomotion. In Beckett's world we are naked spectators of a psychophysical machine — our combination of mind and body and by extension the universe — which capriciously functions or malfunctions without reference to our wishes. That seemed to be my world too this afternoon. The eponymous protagonist of Beckett's novel, *Molloy*, crosses a gloomy forest. His progress is painfully slow because his crutches sink up to the fork in the black slush of fallen leaves on the forest floor. Resting, flat on his face, he strikes his brow.

'Christ, there's crawling', he cries, 'I never thought of that'.

But could he crawl, with his legs in such a state? Flat on his belly, using his crutches like grapnels, he plunges them ahead, fishing for a hold in the undergrowth, and pulls himself forward.

So now I struck my brow and cried, 'Thank you, Sam', turning on to my front and slithering off the bed to begin the crawl to the phone. I was in a bad way but I had scored for the relevance of literature. My hands were spades digging me, brutish and deformed, across the floor to the clumping theme you gave Caliban in your music for *The Tempest*.

The doctor arrived before I'd completed my return crawl back to the bedroom. He got me to my feet and steered me to the bed. My hands and knees were sore from the journey.

'It's encephalitis', he said. 'They used to call it sleeping sickness'.

'Why is there so much light?' I asked him. 'It hurts'.

He went to the window and drew the curtains. I told him about the horses.

'You've got double vision', he said. 'Light is painful because your eyes can't contract and dilate normally in response to degrees of brightness. Keep the curtains drawn'.

He took a syringe from his bag and injected the serum into my left buttock. There was a pungent, cloying smell.

'That's vitamin B complex', he said. 'It's the only way we've got to fight this. There's no real cure for encephalitis. It's a virus, like polio, but this will help to keep your system strong. We'll hope for the best. This will take some time. I'll come every day to give you the injection'.

When he'd gone I looked over at the horses, their white porcelain faintly glimmering across the darkened room. Then I looked at my hands and saw four.

'Specky', echoed jeering voices from the school playground, 'Four Eyes, Four Eyes, Four Eyes'.

Two Douglases stood at the foot of the bed. They wore swastika arm-bands.

'Stand back to back wi' us', they leered, spitting on their hands.

Before I fell asleep twin Margarets came down from the ceiling.

'Master', they invited with wide-angle smiles, '*show* us your *kwela*'.

***

The doctor was right. It took a while — two months in the curtained bedroom. The hallucinations stopped but double vision continued so I took to wearing a black patch over one eye and lay on the bed like a ship-wrecked pirate beached on a desert island. When I wasn't asleep I listened mainly to the Sixth Symphony and chamber music.

Taking a holistic approach to my problem, the doctor set up a record player on the bedside table with a stack of LPs.

'More Vitamin B', he said. 'B for Beethoven. I've brought you the late Quartets. These are prescribed', putting a record on the turntable to play the all-comprehend*ing andante* theme and variations of Opus 131.

'The composer for me above all others is Beethoven', you once said, Sibelius. 'He is a revelation to me. He was a Titan. Everything was against him and yet he triumphed'.

'So show me *how*, Beethoven', I thought.

While still prone I simulated action by plunging into the vortex of the 'Grosse Fuge', originally intended as the finale for Opus 130. This must be the wildest, grandest fugue ever composed, consummation of Beethoven's contrapuntal writing, the most radical, *avant-garde* work by the most formidable composer in history.

Oscar Kokoschka told Schoenberg, 'Your cradle was Beethoven's "Grosse Fuge"', but I refuse to blame Beethoven for the birth of the tone-row and its esoteric spawn of yawps and squonks.

Behind the closed curtains the bedroom windows were open, so you and Beethoven spilled into the street. In breaks between the movements or when I was turning over the LP I could hear the Xhosa voices of passing Africans on the pavement outside. They'd stop at the window to consider the music.

'Thyini thiza!' (Goodness gracious me!) A woman's voice.

'Benzani aba belungu? Tsi! Ingathi bayageza' (What are these whites doing? Golly! It seems they are mad!) Another woman, laughing.

Then the slow voice of a man who'd heard something of my plight: *'Awu! Lendoda imamele kuba kaloku ayibona yimfama'* (Ah, that man listens because he cannot see.)

My centre-piece was a rare LP of The Budapest Quartet's pioneering 1933 record of your Opus 56, the String Quartet you called *Voces Intimae*.

'I have left the training ship and gained my master's certificate', you wrote in your diary on 27 July 1909, 'Now I shall set course for the open sea'.

You'd just completed *Voces Intimae*, or 'Intimate voices', your chamber-music masterpiece. The diary entry is evidence of the incubus of self-doubt that always weighed on you when composing. How else could an artist with your achievements of the previous fifteen years think of himself as a mere trainee until now? The Finnish cult of Sibelius had begun with the first performance of the *Kullervo Symphony* in 1892. Your works included *En Saga*, the *Karelia* music, *The Four Legends from the Kalevala*, some of your finest songs, three symphonies and the Violin Concerto. You had become an essential part of Finnish national history. And still self-doubt.

The String Quartet dramatises tension between self-doubt and determination to face the world, so it spoke directly to my predicament.

The violin doesn't want to be alone in the dark any more than I did.

'Is anyone there?' it asks rather plaintively.

'Yes, it's all right', answers the cello, 'I'm here'.

Contact made, the instruments blend their voices. They discuss and meditate together with increasing intensity, questioning, protesting and accepting. The second movement is so short you called it 'movement first-and-a-half'. Its voices chatter busily, an escapist foil to the thoughtful flow of the first movement, and abruptly fall silent in deference to the elegiac *adagio*. It was in the score for this third movement that you wrote the words *'Voces Intimae'*. There's thanksgiving in this impassioned music as well as lament for what the poet, Wordsworth, calls 'fallings from us, vanishings'. Sinews are stiffened in the robust, extrovert theme of the fourth movement, preparing us for the explosive virtuosity of the finale. The energy is impressive but can't conceal a hint of protesting too much, of whistling in the dark that you would confront more fully a year later in the Fourth Symphony. It's the 'intimate voices' of the ruminative, ambiguous *adagio* which dominate the work. These are the voices which most of all kept me going in a curtained room in Africa. They were my *kwela*. Another of your rescues, Big Man.

***

By the time my eyes could process light again I had recovered the sense of balance. With the piratical patch over one eye navigation returned to normal. I savoured the pleasure of walking through doors without veering uncontrollably into walls. The doctor couldn't promise release from double vision. He thought I had a fifty-fifty chance. Some people were lucky.

Apart from the Sixth Symphony's draughts of cold spring water I hadn't listened to orchestral music in the curtained bedroom and promised myself I'd gorge on big sound when I was well enough to reach the ampler acoustic of the living room. In a letter from Glasgow my father wrote about his enjoyment of the Fifth Symphony. This was a major concession, as he knew I would realize.

Shortly before leaving school I'd lent our treasured 78s of the Second Symphony to a classmate. He'd heard me blethering about you so much that, like my father before him, he grew curious and wanted to find out what this Sibelius could do. He kept the records for several weeks until, in the 'Ol' Man River' tradition, he broke one of the shellac discs by sitting on it and insisted on giving me money for a new set. I didn't want to accept the money because, as my mother would have said, it was an accident and the purpose of the loan had been achieved. I'd made a convert. But he was adamant, so I took the money and went to the record shop. Instead of buying another Second, which I knew by heart, I used the money for an LP of the Fifth Symphony which I wanted to know better. My father sulked when he learned I'd traded in his favourite symphony, though he still hummed the Second during his morning shave. Then he began to enjoy the Fifth. When he discovered that the Symphony was premièred on 8th December 1915, your fiftieth birthday, he put silly words to the theme of the second movement while he helped my mother with housework.

'Oh, now I'm fifty', he sang above the baritone groans of the vacuum, 'I know I'm fifty, because I'm fifty, the Big Man's fifty, oh yes, I'm fifty…'

So my father and I had another meeting place, but I didn't quite believe he'd forgiven my treachery towards the Second until he sent the letter. I had the original LP with me in South Africa, so I knew he'd bought a copy for himself to listen to in Glasgow.

I invented a morning ritual. You do that sort of thing in Africa.

'Pure fuckin' magic', Colossus had said in the 'Duke of Argyll'.

That was a sign that you would be my witch-doctor. The Vitamin B team needed reinforcements. You were a doctor in Helsinki, a doctor at Yale. Now you would be my medicine man in Africa. Doctor Big

Man. My father's letter was another sign, perfectly timed. It was obvious. The Fifth Symphony was the spell that would cure the double vision. No problem, as they say these days.

This was the ritual. At 8.30 a.m. I switched on the record player in the living room, turned up the volume and began to play the LP of the Fifth Symphony. While the opening horn call heralded a journey, I walked to the dining table and sat facing the record player but carefully looking down at the table. I took off the patch, then looked up across the room at the record player's rectangular grille. There were two grilles, two record players. I replaced the patch, walked to the player and lifted the pick-up from the LP. Then I ate breakfast in despondent silence. That was the first day, the second, the third and the twentieth.

I stuck to the ritual. The right time to play the whole record would come when the Symphony had cured the double vision. You and the Symphony were in charge. I must be patient for the magic to do its work.

In the frustration of waiting I remembered that the gestation of the Fifth had been monumentally slow and painful for you. In my mind, there in Africa, our frustrations coincided. You wanted to make the Symphony; I longed to hear it. Of your seven symphonies you struggled most with the Fifth, working on it from summer 1914 to its final version in 1919 and publication in 1921. In June 1914 you returned to Finland from a triumphant month in the USA and began to sketch themes for the Fifth and Sixth Symphonies, experimentally transferring material from one to the other. It was a time of unprecedented international turmoil and volatility in the arts. Russia's political oppression of Finland was severe and the First World War isolated Finland from Europe. Filippo Marinetti had published the *Futurist Manifesto* in 1909, the year in which Mahler completed *Das Lied von der Erde*. Arnold Schoenberg had written his huge symphonic cantata, *Gurrelieder* and was now composing atonal music. In 1913 Stravinsky's *Le Sacre du Printemps* had caused a sensation in Paris. The Finnish architect Eliel Saarinen had designed a bold new building for Helsinki's Central Station. In painting the talk was of Picasso, Chagall, Braque, Kandinsky, Malevich and Duchamp. In the arts everywhere the *avant-garde* clamoured for new forms.

Your five-year struggle with the 5th Symphony was because you wanted the content of the music to determine its form. The authoritative mould of the sonata was now *passé*, but you never relinquished your belief in the necessary rigours of form. The problem you faced was like the difficulty of writing *vers libre*, which, as T.S. Eliot knew, was never really libre, never truly free to the good poet. Now, like a poet, the composer had to devise an appropriate form for each new work; it was no longer available off-the-peg. By the middle of 1918 you were still revising the Fifth Symphony while developing the Sixth and beginning on the Seventh. You had abundant content; the problem was form and the three works required different solutions. How many movements were right for the content of these symphonies? The Sixth took shape in four; the Seventh packed into one evolving arc; the Fifth settled into three.

Magic doesn't like being monitored. When I stopped counting the days it began to work. In the morning ritual position at the dining table I removed the eye patch once again and looked at the grille of the record player. Expectant woodwind motives were answering the horn summons at the start of the Fifth Symphony.

172

There was only one grille. Seconds later it split into two. I stopped the music but began to hope I might be one of the lucky ones. Next morning there was one grille for some seconds more and the following morning for longer still before it reverted to the tormenting double. I heard a little more of the Symphony every day. So, by gradual, teasing increments double became single and stayed that way.

Now I could play the whole Symphony to confirm the power of your magic. I turned up the volume to fill the living room as the first movement found its voices in a profusion of thematic cells, life's abundance, the embryonic horn call sharply echoed by trumpet and flute, confirming the symphony's germinal idea. A mournful bassoon laments desolations of wars and dark rooms. With unifying energy the music confronts nature's enigmas and grandeurs. A chatter of strings and woodwind initiates acceleration into a trumpeted re-statement of the horn call and the pace quickens again. 'To travel hopefully is a better thing than to arrive' says Robert Louis Stevenson, 'and the true success is to labour'. Maybe so, but you've laboured on this music for five years, Sibelius; now it's time for well-earned arrival. Trumpets fanfare once more. Urged on by brass over arpeggio violins the movement races home. Characteristic Sibelian clouds menace but can't suppress my father's chirpy, appropriating song, now inseparable from the tender tune at the heart of the second movement; but can we hear, behind the smile, something a little wry about the solitude of the artist like the loneliness in Elgar's 'Enigma' theme? The abrupt ending of this movement is your way of saying 'pay attention, there's more to come', alerting us to the next, concluding stage of your argument. Here it comes: the apocalyptic lyricism of the swinging horn theme which you called 'the incomparable swan hymn'. You'd been inspired by the sight of sixteen swans in flight: 'Nature's mystery and life's Angst', you wrote in your diary, as if paraphrasing the ambiguous chords of the most astonishing of all symphonic endings.

Sibelius, that morning in Africa your hymn wasn't only for a white man's mended vision but for Margaret too. Perhaps I dared hope she'd forgiven me. Wherever she was, I prayed she was gracing someone with her incandescent smile. I hoped she was listening to Spokes. I hoped she'd remember you.

It was over. Doctor Big Man had delivered. Colossus was waving from the 'Duke of Argyll'.

'Told you, pal. Magic'.

***

South Africa was already so evidently changed and open in 1992 that the name of the library at Johannesburg's Rand Afrikaans University came as a shock, a jackboot kick from the murderous past. Above the entrance were the words, 'H.F. Verwoerd Biblioteek'. 'Get that name off that building', I snapped at the kind man who was showing me round. Members of the university's academic staff approached me later and said they'd heard I'd been offended by the name of the library. They were upset too, so would I please write and say so to their Rector? I did, first thanking him for my enjoyable visit to his institution, then continuing:

> *My pleasure in the occasion was a little modified by the shock of finding that the University's library still bears the name of H.F. Verwoerd. The impact on a visitor of this name of all names cannot, I believe, be other than damaging to the University's*

international image. To many people a
comparable situation would be the similar
commemoration of Hitler by a German
university... I realise, of course, that such a
matter can easily enough be overlooked in
a rapidly changing environment, but may I
recommend that the name be removed? I make
the recommendation most respectfully and out
of tenderness towards a country for which I
have the deepest affection.

No reply from the Rector.

Yet part of the world's duty towards South Africa is to develop informed sympathy for the Afrikaner people who have no other home and whose complex fate is not simply reducible to Ezekiel Mphahlele's definition of the South African Parliament as 'a bunch of lawless Voortrekker descendants whose safety [lay] in the hands of sten-gun-happy police youngsters'. Every human group has its thugs. I was bound to be moved by the moral courage of an Afrikaner who told me what it had been like to live under the spell of Verwoerd. She remembered his visiting her school, the charisma of his personality and the impact he made by touching every pupil. She confessed that, when a man who thought he was doing too much for coloured people stabbed him to death on 6 September 1966 as he sat on his bench in Parliament waiting for the day's business to begin, she felt as though the world had come to an end with the demise of the nation's great white father. In 1960 he had lain in a hospital bed recovering from the first attempt to kill him.

'I heard the shots and then I realized that I could still think', he told his wife. 'And I knew that I had been spared to complete my life's work'.

Ever since then the Afrikaner *volk* had regarded

176

Grahamstown, showing the African location on the hill

his recovery as proof that God had chosen him as His divine instrument to forge the South African nation. He'd been guarding the racial purity of his people since 1936 when he organized a group of professors at the University of Stellenbosch to protest against the admission to South Africa of a shipload of Jews fleeing from Nazi Germany. The government reaffirmed its faith in *apartheid* before his blood had been cleaned from the floor of Parliament. In the Zambian legislature laughter broke out when the assassination was announced. God had changed his mind.

Only in the 1970s did my Afrikaner friend begin to realise that Verwoerd – and she – had been profoundly wrong. Now she had a true moral position from which to say, on the site of a Boer War concentration camp in Potchefstroom where Afrikaner women and children had died of starvation and cruelty, 'Don't forget, the concentration camp was a British invention'.

Standing in Grahamstown's High Street, reading a newspaper, I noticed that I'd been spotted by an old African man about 20 feet away and saw him begin to walk towards me. He came up slowly, stopped with his back to me and half-turned.

'Master', he said, 'I'm looking for money'.

I said nothing. He shuffled.

Again, 'Master, I'm looking for money'.

Still I didn't look at him and said nothing. Long pause.

'Master ...'

I shook my head, feeling again the mutually demeaning frustration and anger of the familiar situation, and said, 'No'.

The old rationale came back: if you give to one beggar you'll have a crowd of them at you. This is the State's problem, not mine. And now, since the revoking of the Pass Laws, on the hillside above the town were some 40,000 black squatters who had come in from the country to look for work in a town where there is no industry. Should I give to him and not to them?

He sighed. 'Master, I'm trying to go home'.

That did it. I looked into his eyes, the same eyes as thirty years ago, the same eyes as a hundred or three hundred years ago, the face of a melancholy turtle. I gave him all the change in my pocket and, as he went slowly away, remembered Margaret's going and felt ashamed for not giving more.

In a shop in the same town a friendly Xhosa man explained the origins of merchandise.

'This is Ndebele, this is Xhosa, this is made by white people in factory'.

I asked him if he could understand what I was about to say and unlocked my tiny word-hoard of Xhosa.

'*Ufudo lwakho olunoqhoqhoqho obuhlungu lusela amanzi am*'.

'Yes', he said at once, 'you say my tortoise with the sore throat is drinking your water', jack-knifing into a seismic laugh and coming out of it to clasp my hand across decades of oppression.

This is the miracle, Sibelius, after the agony. First and Third worlds meeting, choosing not to perish but to negotiate, touching.

I spoke on the telephone to Vivian, the African maid who came when I lost Margaret. She began the conversation by calling me 'Master' in the old way, but to my delight ended by using my first name. That couldn't have happened in the sick time. Another phone call put me in touch with Peter Kotha, a Professor at the University of Fort Hare. In 1964, when he was a student, I taught him Shakespeare furtively, mainly the comedies. My house was two doors away from the police station. Peter would come in by the back door after dark. When our session was finished he wouldn't let me take him home. I would drive him to a place from which he would zig-zag his way back to the location on his own. Such was the fear of being harassed by the police or Special Branch because of his association with a white known to be a Liberal. Now, 28 years later, he was on top of his life.

'Ah, my brother', he said, 'I am a Professor of Education now, so you see what comes from Much Ado about Nothing!'

At the University of the Orange Free State in Bloemfontein I gave a talk about literature at a Festival of English for school pupils sponsored by SASOL, the South African Synthetic Oil company. When I looked down from the platform and saw in 350 upturned faces all the colours of South Africa together at last the impulse was to weep. No more the sick double vision of *apartheid*, splitting the beloved country into whites and non-whites. In this land of tragedy and enchantment the magic of the human spirit was prevailing against fearful odds. Through a sequence of short, accessible poems I encouraged the children to think of poems as songs. Finally I invited them to sing a poem-song with me. Nothing as lofty as your *Song of the Athenians*, Sibelius, which would have been ideal for the historical moment, or the verses of the *Finlandia Anthem*, just a popular song by the Scottish group, The Proclaimers. Dividing the children into two teams I rehearsed the refrain of the song with each team in turn. A tape of the song got them started and competition with the recording drew more and more volume from the half-laughing, half-singing voices of the children to the end of the

179

Children of the location, Kenton-on-Sea, near Grahamstown

Township shack, Bophuthatswana, near Sun City

song when the climax was cheering, clapping and stamping:

> *But I would walk 500 miles*
> *And I would walk 500 more*
> *Just to be the man who walked 1000 miles*
> *To fall down at your door.*

In the happy babble when the singing finished I stepped in front of the lectern and gave them the freedom fist. It was given back with a roar. These children of South Africa knew, like the defiant Soweto school-children of 1976 memorialised in the 1987 black musical *Sarafina*, that if complete freedom from the past was still to come, it was 'coming tomorrow'. Their rooms had been dark for decades; now the curtains were flung open and light was flooding in. Their Douglases were down and out.

Apartheid died on 11 February 1990 when F. W. de Klerk's National Government released Nelson Mandela from prison and unbanned the resistance movements. On one level, as a former member of the Liberal Party I could only be jubilant to find that the hellish system was in ashes at last. Underground resistance could come, blinking, into the light of a new political day without fear of interrogation, torture, bullets and bombs. Mandela's indefatigable supporters who had kept his cause alive for so many years in London's Trafalgar Square could go home at last and recede into normal lives from their valorous labours on behalf of the would-be moral world. Bless them and let them clasp their loved ones, knowing the good they've done.

Aside from Zulu/Xhosa rivalry, extreme right-wing reaction to reform and the inevitable chicaneries the real problem now would be the immemorial one of

183

184

'Block AK 47', Durban

Disraeli's two nations, rich and poor. How could a country as economically split as Brazil between middle class and underclass raise the quality of life for its disadvantaged millions in a world of corporate greed and remorseless profiteering? On another level I was continuously tense in terms of the new, non-political violence in the new milieu. There was a squatter camp in Durban known as 'Block AK 47'. Camps of the poor and powerless surrounded every city, hungry people living in shanties made of oil drums and tarpaulin, tyres, sacks, cardboard boxes, radiator grilles, scrap. Even a brand new black government can't bring down bread from heaven. The dawn of democracy was already accelerating the downward slide of poor whites, living at last the reality they were sheltered from by *apartheid*. Mandela has brought his people emancipation from political bondage; but there are still bondages of poverty, misunderstanding, graft and violence. There are record-breaking statistics for murders, rapes, burglaries, car hi-jackings. South Africa is believed to have the most severe HIV epidemic in the world. Transitional setbacks are inevitable but there is scope for progress now and hope for my beloved Margaret wherever she might be. Hope's out in the open. Under *apartheid* it was imprisoned, tortured, thrown from high police windows, forced under ground or, like Thabo Mbeki, into exile.

And when people complain about corruption, cronyism and patronage in the new régime we should remember what Edmund Burke said: 'Example is the school of mankind and they will learn at no other'. Our response must be swift and incisive.

'We taught them by example'.

May the example of Nelson Mandela prevail. We look at our burning world and know we need help. Let's learn from Madiba.

186

Table Mountain

Amandla! Ubuntu! Nkosi Sikelel i'Afrika.

The power of the land came clamorously back, especially the huge brown and blue spaces of the Transvaal, the bony magic of the bush — among its fabulous creatures a springbok arced high, airborne for a breath-taking second — and the sovereign mass of Table Mountain, pure Fifth Symphony. I remembered going back to Britain in 1965 and feeling as choked by its greenery as by its muddled, archaic politics and the failures of socialism. There is much to be said for the fiery assertions of aloes and proteas and the thorn-trees of the bush. Leaving Africa I left a candour of earth and element and memories of my cure by Doctor Big Man. As South African Airways flight 280 took me up and away from that wondrous, ancient earth I thought of Juluka's question, 'African sky blue, will you bless my life?' and felt there could be no more authenticating blessing. At 30,000 feet Ex. 19 filled my mind. An answer to the child's prayer seemed, at last, possible.

7. America

Under a leaden sky in July 1965 the *Cape Town Castle* docked at Southampton after three weeks of temperamental ocean, gulls and flying fish. There had been a short stop at Las Palmas, where you could see poor people moving in and out of concrete-coloured caves, apparently worse off than Margaret in the Grahamstown location. The practicalities of departure had been a distraction from the sadness of leaving South Africa. Empty sea numbed the immediate sense of loss. The sea wasn't anywhere except itself, so during the voyage there was nothing to compare with the place I'd lived in so intensely for three years. Suddenly there were crowds of irrelevant, pale-faced people talking in voices which had become alien though they spoke my own language, streets without Xhosa women carrying babies on their backs, no piccanins swapping grins and cheek for tickies. The earth smelled wrong. I'd belonged to this country once; now it was no more mine than the one I'd loved and abandoned. Too late I knew I'd been unfaithful to both and now had neither. If life was a staircase I was stubbing my toes on too many risers. I had followed too much the devices and desires of my muddled heart and there was no health in me.

Vivian knew I was making a mistake. After the enveloping hug when I said good-bye she wiped her eyes with her apron, then wagged an admonitory finger.

'You will be *udla ukutya kokuhamba*', she warned. I would be 'one who eats the food of the road', with no fixed residence, always on the move.

Glasgow University had invited me back to Scotland to join its constellation of geniuses as a lecturer in English. I suspected a clerical error but not for me to

189

reason why, only to be grateful for leaving *apartheid* while shaking in my shoes at the prospect of facing again the scathing incredulity of John Oldrid Scott's grimy neo-Gothic tower.

'What's this? Back again? Well, you'll have to prove yourself now, young man.'

The trouble was I'd become more thrall to American than English literature. Anthony Trollope summed up the difference between the two.

'The creations of American literature generally are no doubt more given to the speculative – less given to the realistic – than are those of English literature. On our side of the water we deal more with beef and ale, and less with dreams'.

South African police-state realities generated dreams, mainly Nelson Mandela's rainbow-republic vision of a barely imaginable democratic future. Dreams stayed with you longer than beef and ale, so while lecturing on the great books of Eng. Lit. in the tradition of the Department which had taught them to me, I was privately relishing Emerson and Thoreau, Hawthorne and Melville, Whitman, Emily Dickinson and William Faulkner. I wanted to bring them into the curriculum.

'Ridiculous', boomed the relentless tower. 'What a nerve. How can you profess American literature if you've never been to America?'

America was an intimidating prospect in the 1960s for a boy from Anniesland Cross with a lingering post-war Scottish sense of cultural mediocrity. The wars in Korea and Vietnam had dented the country's moral stature, but it was still the richest, most confident and powerful nation on earth. Milk and honey seemed to flow in abundance as if the river of prosperity had run unchecked since the fifties when, according to Bill Bryson, it was the most gratifying place in history to be alive, a Norman Rockwell utopia of Frigidaires, Chevrolets with Triple-Turbine Turbo-Glide, leafy suburbs, Superman, milk from contented cows, family. A far cry from the urban wastelands and dour high-rise concrete housing schemes of Glasgow. The Soviet Union slipped in its arrogant card to compound the sense of inferiority. America got Aleksandr Solzhenitsyn and Glasgow, for a few days, got Ovidily ('Call me Ovid') Gorchakov.

Comrade Gorchakov made it clear to those of us convened to meet him under the auspices of the Scottish Arts Council that he wasn't much interested in anyone 'who cannot help me with my project'. His project appeared to be a historical novel involving the Scottish forebears of Mikhail Lermontov. If this bespoke a singleness of purpose at odds with the larger issues of cultural *détente,* there was, nevertheless, something undeniably impressive about Mr Gorchakov's conception of himself as a hero of his times. He certainly talked big.

'I write altogether fourteen books', he said.

'My goodness me, that's an awful lot of books', said Lavinia Derwent, creator of Tammy Troot (a fish for children, fractionally less renowned than the Loch Ness Monster), 'How on earth do you manage so many at the one time? Is it pills you take?'

'Naw', said Mr Gorchakov with an intonation and scoop of the head cribbed from Eisenstein's Ivan the Terrible, 'naw. We are socialist country, not capitalist country'.

'Of course', said Miss Derwent, making at once the connection between capitalism and decadent stimulants.

'In my country', said Mr Gorchakov, 'my books make fifty thousand, one hundred thousand copies'.

'Goodness', said Miss Derwent, imprecisely.

'Oh yes, oh yes. All over the place. When I translate into languages of our many republics I get thirty per cent of original contract'.

'How nice'.

'Oh yes, oh yes. We are socialist country. If we were capitalist country, with all my books I would be already MILLINER'.

'Right enough', said Miss Derwent, 'I'm sure you would'.

Tammy Troot had sabotaged the bullying pretensions of the Russian Bear (thereby earning your applause, surely, Sibelius). Scotland 1, USSR nil. If we could score like that against the Soviet Union, America shouldn't be a problem.

You don't argue with the tower, Sibelius. To America I went with the principal object of learning as much as possible about the Southern writer, Robert Penn Warren, destined to become the country's first Poet Laureate. He had stepped into my personal anthology with some early poems and a novel, All the King's Men, and showed every sign of staying. His papers were at Yale University, so I followed you to New Haven, Connecticut, 54 years after you'd gone there to receive the University's award of an Honorary Doctorate of Music at a ceremony on 17th June 1914.

On the morning of the ceremony you forgot breakfast.

'I was so excited about the degree and so fearful lest I should make some blunder, that I have been absent minded all the morning!'

Heads turned to watch you set off from your hotel to the Yale campus resplendent in a black silk robe topped by the green and black hood of the University of Helsinki's Doctor of Philosophy. There was a stately procession to Woolsey Hall, the University's auditorium. There, while the audience were seating themselves, Horatio Parker, Professor of Music, conducted an orchestra in passages from *Finlandia*, *Valse Triste* and *Spring Song*. When it was time to confer your degree you walked to the centre of the platform and stood listening as the citation was read to the assembly:

> *By his music intensely national in inspiration and yet sympathy with the mood of the West, Dr. Sibelius long since captured Finland, Germany, and England, and on coming to America to conduct a Symphonic Poem, found that his fame had already preceded him here also. Still in the prime of life, he has become, by the power and originality of his work one of the most distinguished of living composers. What Wagner did with Teutonic legend, Dr Sibelius has done in his own impressive way with the legends of Finland as embodied in her national epic. He has translated the Kalevala into the universal language of music, remarkable for its breadth, large simplicity, and the infusion of a deeply poetic personality.*

Fitting words, as far as they went, on a grand, happy, deserved occasion, and you savoured 'the prime of life'; but were you, perhaps, disappointed that there was no explicit recognition of how far you had gone beyond programmatic *Kalevala* music in the power and originality of four symphonies, the Violin Concerto and *Voces Intimae*?

You'd also gone to America to earn a fee of $1200 for conducting your own works at the Norfolk Music Festival in Connecticut, created by Carl Stoeckel, the wealthy businessman who had commissioned you to write a new tone poem no more than fifteen minutes long. You'd been working on a score provisionally called 'Rondo of the Waves', but now you gave it the Finnish title *Aallottaret*. We know it as *The Oceanides*, a reference to Hesiod's 'neat-ankled daughters of Oceanus'. It took pride of place in the concert on 4th June performed by a crack orchestra of New York's finest players. Inevitably, it's been compared to Debussy's impressionistic *La Mer*, but your waters are colder, more purely elemental. Where Debussy divides his evocation into three distinct moods, you give us a unified continuity of change. Waves furl and cream, glint in the sun, go black into a metallic mass that heaves and roars before subsiding into provisional calm. Sir Thomas Beecham recorded the work because you asked him to, although he said he thought it a 'strange composition – very strange indeed'. Not strange at all, Big Man: entirely recognizable if you've watched the ocean improvising from lapping, oily swell to roller-coaster candy floss against blank horizons on a voyage from Cape Town to Southampton. Your faithful American apostle, the critic Olin Downes, thought it 'a picture of limitless and eternal power, the finest evocation of the sea which has ever been produced in music', but the tone poem is more than a picture. It's the manifold spirit and magnitude of the sea, with no reference to ankles. In *The Oceanides* you did for the ocean what you would do later for the snowbound forests of the North in *Tapiola*.

You were fêted and garlanded, plied with compliments and caviar at New York's Delmonicos and taken to Niagara Falls.

'The great spectacle is the nearest to true religion of anything I have yet felt', you said, 'and I believe music comes next to it'.

You'd thought of developing your impression of the Falls into a new work, but decided otherwise.

'I have given up the idea', you said. 'It is too solemn and too vast to be represented by any human individual'. But it's tempting to fancy that the magnitude of the Falls may have developed your feeling for scale, affecting the majesties you would compose in your Fifth and Seventh Symphonies.

New York was even more of a wonderland than you'd expected. You'd never been inside a building more than six stories high. When Carl Stoeckel said your apartment in the Essex hotel would be on the tenth floor you couldn't imagine how anyone might sleep at such a height. You slept all right, but the American shower-bath was such a novelty – and New York was so hot that May – you broke your sleep for the refreshment of three cold showers on your first night. Reverse saunas for a Finn.

The size of Grand Central Station astonished you.

'What a place for a concert', you exclaimed, 'if one could have an orchestra of two or three hundred pieces!'

The Indian name of the long Housatonic River delighted you – you repeated it many times so as to memorize it – and the beauty of its 'winds' between New Milford and Canaan. Rehearsals in the Festival's performance venue, 'The Shed', inspired the musicians with enthusiasm and when you raised your baton at the concert for the first measures of *Pohjola's Daughter* there began 'an hour of the most tense and interested attention' Mr Stoeckel had ever known. He thought your conducting graceful and forceful, but you didn't seem to care for the 1,2,3,4 beat. Your motions suggested 'one who was reading a mighty poem'. The audience rose in ovation.

America's recognition and applause were as loud and lavish as the Falls and didn't stop after you'd sailed for home on the *President Grant*. In 1935 a New York Philharmonic Society poll revealed that you'd outstripped all other composers in popularity. But for the outbreak of war, you'd probably have accepted the invitation to make a profitable conducting tour of the country. It must have been partly gratitude to your American friends that brought you out of retirement on New Year's Day 1939 to conduct the Helsinki Grand Radio Concert Orchestra in your *Andante Festivo* for a special broadcast transmitted worldwide as a salute to the World Fair to be held in New York the following summer. Ironically, the broadcast was meant to be a message of peace to a world soon to become more blood-stained than ever before.

This stately hymn-like music is scarcely the drum-and-trumpet fanfare the New York World Fair might have expected by way of a festive salvo. Why this liturgical solemnity? For such an occasion why not choose the last movement of the First or Second or Third or Fifth Symphony? Why not the 'Alla Marcia' from the *Karelia Suite*? Why not remember your happy visit to America with a performance of *The Oceanides*? Why not herald a new era of world peace with the affirming light of your rising sun in *Night Ride and Sunrise*?

Maybe the radio people asked you for *Andante Festivo* because it was the right length for their programme, or possibly the scoring accorded with the instrumentalists available on that day. But perhaps the music of this piece was your way of telling New York and the world that you'd reached a point of repose after a lifetime of effort. You'd gone to the edge of the abyss at the end of the Seventh Symphony and looked into the frozen landscape of *Tapiola*. Now, as James Joyce says of Leopold Bloom, we might say of you: 'He rests. He has travelled'.

196

Could there be a connection between addiction to your music and the singular appeal of Robert Penn Warren's writing? Canonic welcomes may not be rational but you'd expect a pattern, a kinship of proclivities. Warren's narrator in *All the King's Men* says, 'I eat a persimmon and the teeth of a tinker in Tibet are put on edge', but what could link a Finnish composer to a writer, forty years younger, from the American South? Your life began among the comfortable wooden houses and green gardens of nineteenth-century Hämeenlinna. Musical soirées and home concerts were a norm of the town's genial social life before you were born. A cultural galaxy away, on 24th April, 1905 Robert Penn Warren was born in Guthrie, Kentucky. In those days the town prospered as a tobacco market-place and railway junction near the Tennessee border. Now it's left high, dry and defunctive by the tide of progress and 'Thank you for not smoking'. No caviar from Delmonicos down there, Sibelius, no champagne and no evidence of an appetite for classical music among its citizens. A different America from yours. Hominy grits, pork chitterlings, checked shirts and denim, bourbon and branch, country ham and country music.

You'd both have vexed Anthony Trollope's distinction between the worldly and the speculative. Robust consumers of whatever beefs and ales, you both knew that we're all meant to dream. Against all the odds of origin, that's the connection.

After your father died you lived in your Grandmother's house on Prykikatu in Hämeenlinna. The garden of roses, lilac and fruit trees stretched to the shore of Lake Vanajavesi. Down there with other children you played with stones and splashed in the water until you became abstracted, fascinated by the movement of the waves or the reflection

197

of the sun on the lake. When your mother asked why you'd stopped playing you'd tell her you were watching the fairies and fabulous creatures which you then drew, explaining that you'd seen them in unimaginable places. You were a born dreamer. On a wintry afternoon when you were six you didn't come indoors from playing at the usual time before dark, to the consternation of your grown-ups.

'Why are you so late? Where have you been all this time?' asked Granny when you finally showed up looking like a diminutive knight of woeful countenance.

'I've been in a fire', you said. 'There was a big house burning to the ground and lots of people carrying water to throw on the flames and I carried buckets and buckets and I got soaked and my shirt's all wet and I'm terribly cold'.

Your mother called for fresh wood for the stove so that she could warm you up and change your clothes in front of the fire. Everyone was asking where the burning house was but you didn't seem to know, just that it was somewhere near the lakeshore. When the stove was burning brightly your mother began to undress you. None of your garments was wet. Now the grilling began: was there really a burning house and did you really carry all these buckets of water to put out the flames?

'Well, no, I suppose I didn't actually carry water myself, just the other people'.

More questions until you admitted that there hadn't been a real fire at all. You'd been standing by the lakeshore gazing at a house. You imagined what it would be like if the house caught fire and how you'd rush to help.

But the fire was real to you. It wasn't a lie. There are dreams about how the world is and dreams about how the world might be. The burning house was both kinds of dream, a true dream about how your world was and what you wished you could have done to make it different. By the time you were six you understood that your father's death had razed the security of your birthplace and you were old enough to wish that you could have saved it and him. You'd have carried buckets of water until you dropped if you could have kept the dream of your first home intact for your father and mother and sister and you. If Granny's house were to catch fire you'd put out the flames single-handed and save everyone. You were dreaming and telling the truth. Later you would mine the *Kalevala* for dreams of heroism, the hazards of love, the origin of fire and the birth of the world.

For Robert Penn Warren the defining human project is to have a dream and make it come true, to make the poetry of our dreams work in a world of prose and imperfection. In an early poem, 'Bearded Oaks', the dream of love earns its keep by surviving the most inward kinds of opposition, the decay of passion and erosions of time:

> *I do not love you less that now*
> *The caged heart makes iron stroke*
> *Or less that all that light once gave*
> *The graduate dark should now revoke.*

In *All the King's Men* Warren's themes grow from his scrutiny of the career of Huey Long, Governor of Louisiana in the 1930s, whose slogan proclaimed his dream to make 'every man a king'. Like his real-life prototype, Warren's character, Willie Stark, starts off as a popular reformer bent on raising the common people's quality of life and waging war on corrupt

199

Robert Penn Warren

administration. His mission is as pure as Martin Luther King's in a different arena, but, like Long, he degenerates into a rabble-rousing power-seeker. With accelerating megalomaniac sincerity he attacks corruption by corrupt methods and poisons his own dream. His apparently benevolent despotism brings material benefit to the State but is conducted in the interest of his own self-aggrandizement and in a spirit of contempt for the people.

'Man is conceived in sin and born in corruption and he passeth from the stink of the didie to the stench of the shroud'.

This becomes the only truth for Willie, but the dream of virtue lies in wait for him because, as Warren puts it in his long poem, *Brother to Dragons*:

> *... despite all naturalistic considerations*
> *Or in the end because of naturalistic*
> *   considerations,*
> *We must believe in virtue. There is no*
> *Escape. No inland path round that rocky*
> *And spume-nagged promontory. There is no*
> *Escape: dead-fall on trail, noose on track,*
> *   bear-trap*
> *Under the carefully rearranged twigs. There*
> *   is no*
> *Escape, for virtue is*
> *More dogged than Pinkerton, more scientific*
> *   than the FBI,*
> *And that is why you wake sweating towards*
> *   dawn.*

Deny the dream at your peril. At the end, sensing his own incompleteness, Willie gives way to a fatal yearning for virtue, the purity of the egalitarian dream he began with. He builds a free hospital, refusing to allow it to be engulfed in the graft typical of his administration. Too late: the dream has been contaminated by his interpretation of life in terms of corruption. He's assassinated by Adam Stanton, Warren's inflexibly virtuous doctor who will not admit infection into his moral preserve. Stanton, too, is killed. Beauty and the Beast drown in the dream both need but can't realize.

There's a parable about realizing the dream in the last movement of your Second Symphony, Sibelius, if you'll permit a musical theme to represent the idea of the dream. The movement enacts a typically Sibelian pattern which can be heard in all the symphonies, even in the smiling second movement of the Fifth. You find the security of a theme, then depart from it, pushing riskily into surrounding musical territory to check out the environment and measure other potentialities. Maybe you've settled too readily for the certainty of your theme; perhaps your certainty is not sufficiently earned in terms of the way the world is. This is not the same as the classical sonata progression of statement, development and recapitulation, which has built-in security all the way. It's a matter of discovery, risk, test and return. The movement's second subject in F sharp minor is announced by the woodwind over darkly swirling strings and a soft drum roll. This is the dream theme, the ideal. It's so sure and complete that we expect it to rule the music at once, but as the strings rise over a pizzicato figure the music fragments and climbs away from the security of the theme. Can the dream, like the child's prayer, hold its own with the grown-ups? There follows a richly orchestrated melodic sequence and we think this must surely be where we're going. But no. Abruptly there's another change of direction and another song-like passage collapses unresolved. Then a trumpet brings back the dream theme of the second subject. Ah, we begin to relax. Now the options have been tested, risks run and resolution earned. This will be the road taken. The theme is pressed forward to a climax of certainty. All is well. We must not commit what Herman Melville calls 'hideous and intolerable allegory', but this exultant music seems to tell us that if we are to rise to the measure of our potential we must test our dreams in the welter of the world's possibilities. Fulfilment of the dream may be the reward if our effort, like yours, is without stint.

Robert Penn Warren's opinion too.

'Oh no', I might hear you cry in horror, Sibelius, 'I did not intend such meanings to be found in this music'.

Yes, my fable may look far-fetched, though I hope it doesn't offend; but, as Henry James reminds us, 'Really, universally, relations stop nowhere' and Mr Stoeckel said you told the Americans that everyone must use his or her own imagination for your works. Doesn't that give a junky equal rights with a critic?

8. A smuggler's songs and silence on the margin

Daughter Charlotte was almost six when she asked what the music was.

'It's called Symphony No. 3'.

'What's sifny?' I explained.

'It's nice', she said. The second movement was playing.

'The man who wrote it is called Sibelius'.

'Siblus', she tried, 'Siblyblusayus', now a bundle of giggles on her back on the floor.

'No, not quite. Si-be-li-us'.

She sat up, puckered her face, took the name and possessed it.

'Sib-ay-lee-US!' she cried, jumping up, 'Sib-ay-lee-US!, the last syllable a gleeful whoop.

The tune stuck as it had so many years ago to me.

After South Africa there was divorce. Charlotte came to me at week-ends. They were difficult times, Sibelius, but you always helped. 'No. 3' was a fixture. I told her about the prayer and Granny's idea of a child entering a room of grown-ups on tiptoe and she'd ask me to tell her again. With the record playing she'd leave the room, close the door, pause for a giggle, open the door and tiptoe back in, accelerating across the room into my arms, my chum, growing fast.

It was always sore when I had to take her home to her mother's. Then, when she was nine, she ran away.

The red blur was her sweater behind the frosted glass of the front door. Her fist went in and out of focus, hammering on the pane. She stumbled in like a wounded bird, head down and to the side. Her right hand reached for my neck as her body balled into my arms.

'Daddy. Oh, Daddy, Daddy'.

There were no bruises. The *News of the World* wouldn't have been interested and she wasn't game for a social worker. The social workers had their hands full in Easterhouse, Blackhill, the city's trouble spots. West-End problems were expected to solve themselves. A West-End girl of nine, with all her advantages, had to be wilful, perverse. But she'd only been five when the divorce came through. I'd sung to her nearly every night until I made the break. She loved Kipling's 'A Smuggler's Song'. Maybe the singing had stunted her growth.

Now, the front door of the flat still swinging open in the wind that funnelled up from the close-mouth, she huddled into me.

'Can we play No. 3?'

I'd called her in Glasgow from a phone box near the Yale University library.

'Hey, how's my old parcel?'

The endearment, backfiring into a tearful gulp, nearly wrecked the whole thing. The just deserts of sentimentality. A father who walks out on his child isn't entitled to be sentimental. It confuses the child. But it wasn't Charlotte I'd left, she must know that. Born into a marriage of true impediments, she had come, like a consolation prize, an unexpected parcel. Consolation hadn't been enough to hold me, but I'd come back, I would, and she'd have two homes instead of just one.

'How's it going?' I said into the telephone.

'Fine'.

'What did you do today, Parcel?'

'I was playing in the garden. I got new sandals. Daddy?'

'Yes, Parcel'.

'Say the name'.

'Sibelius'.

'Sib-ay-lee-US!'

'That's right, Parcel. What time is it over there?'

'Almost eight. Mummy says I'm having a bath tonight'.

'Bet you fall asleep in five seconds after a day in the garden and a bath'.

'Daddy, hum No. 3'.

'Ta-ra-*rum*-pum-pum-ta-ra-ra-ra-*raa-ra*'. Then a cough to cover the shakes.

'Daddy, I miss you'. Tears were close now.

'I miss you too, Parcel'. Oh, come on Daddy, come on. Get love along the line. Give her something she can use. 'Listen, you're going to bed in a wee while?'

'Yes, Daddy'.

'Let's sing the song, okay?'

'Okay'. A smile in the voice; she'd got the message. It would need to be soft but very clear if we were to hear each other in duet. Point consonants, easy on sibilants. Pauses between the lines to allow for the time-lag of long distance.

'Right. I'll start. We'll do the refrain. Ready?'

'Yes, Daddy'.

'Okay. Five and twenty ponies, Trotting through the dark, Brandy for the parson, Baccy for the clerk, Laces for the lady', I paused.

'...Laces for the lady', Charlotte sang.

'Letters for the spy, And watch the wall, my darling, While the gentlemen go by'.

What would Kipling have thought of this use of his song? Smuggling love into the enemy camp? What did you and Granny think, Sibelius, about this use of your No. 3?

'Daddy, that was lovely. I've got to go for my bath now'.

'Good night, old Parcel'.

***

I closed the front door, took her to the sitting room, hushing the sobs, put No. 3 on the turntable, brought the tone-arm in to the second movement, sat her on my lap and felt the tension slip from her body with the lilt of the child's prayer.

For some time she'd been hinting on the weekly access visits that she'd like to live with me.

'They don't like me', she said of her mother and step-father. 'They whisper to each other'.

Recently, when it was time to go home, she had hidden under a bed or in a closet, gingerly feeling along the line that separated mischief from getting her point over. Now she had run nearly two miles in sweater and skirt on a dripping winter's night. A Saturday, just on pub-closing.

'Daddy, I had to come home'.

Drops of rain ran from her hair. She shivered as her engine wound down.

She had planned her escape. It was a kind of seediness she was rejecting, nothing criminal. Morning tempers, the four-letter words that spiked adult sarcasms, a stack of Danish pornography glimpsed in a cupboard, the punctilious appearance at dinner of the carefully chilled Sauvignon Blanc or chambréd Merlot yet the failure of clean socks and underwear to arrive in her drawer with comparable regularity until she'd learned to wash them herself by hand.

'My panties are always grey', she said, 'I never get them white when I wash them'.

Well, they wouldn't club her to death with grey panties, but they were colouring her view with them.

208

With her mother's attention on preparations for the evening's lasagna and her step-father attending to television, she had gone upstairs to her room. She liked the room because it was small, her cocoon, except on windy nights, like tonight, when branches of trees along the back lane would sweep across the big streetlamp. Sinister flickerings and twisted shadow shapes pushed through the curtains on to her bed. She concentrated on packing her duffel bag. There were clothes and the school things. Going to school from Daddy's would tell everyone that his house was her everyday, not just her week-end home.

'Sib-ay-lee-US', she said to the bag.

The weight of the bag surprised her and when she got it downstairs to the basement the rope was hurting her hand. She set it on the floor and took down her school raincoat from the pegs in the passage. With the coat over her arm she heaved up the duffel bag by its rope and found she was trembling. The back door still had to be opened. She put the bag down again and dumped the coat on top. The big door was sticky with damp and she had to pull on the handle with both hands.

Wind gusted in at her and the wildly flickering lamp in the lane forced her back into the doorway like a prisoner dodging a spotlight. She couldn't face the back way as planned. She would have to travel light. Leaving the duffel bag and coat where they were, a lumpy cairn by the door, she turned and ran up the stairs to the ground floor, flinching at the sound of television as she passed the closed door of the sitting room. Movement made her feel better. She opened the front door. As she closed it and caught the rain and wind on her face, she let out a yelp of jubilation.

At first she was conscious only of her motion as she ran. Faces ballooned out of the darkness and were left behind.

'Sib-ay-lee-US, Sib-ay-lee-US', she chanted in time to her running.

The smell of wet wool rose at her from her sweater and she thought it was funny how the cold rain turned warm when it touched her. A group of drinkers outside a pub stared at her. A drunk on the other side of the street waved jerkily.

'Aw ma wee darlin' – didyi go an' miss yer bus? Is that no' rotten?'

Daddy's song about the smugglers came into her head and she fell into its rhythm. 'Five and twenty ponies, Trotting through the dark'. The last stretch was downhill but she had a stitch in her side. She couldn't stop because the lasagna would be ready now, they'd have looked for her and know she'd gone. They'd be after her. She wanted to cry but couldn't do that and run at the same time. She promised herself she'd cry later. Daddy's tenement was at the next corner, red sandstone walls slick in the rain, a glistening fortress.

***

Lawyer McLaren was home, snug in suburbia, when I rang.

'Basically, in law, the child's place is with the mother since she has custody', he said. 'It would probably be best for the child if her mother would agree to allow her to remain in your house for tonight, but, logically, it would be quite wrong to approve what the child has done or to give her the impression that she can just decide to take up her abode with you. The fact that the child has absconded from her mother's house changes nothing, basically'.

I put the phone down, then dialled the number of the house from which Charlotte and I had both fled.

'You will return her within half an hour', said her mother.

'My lawyer thinks it would be better if you let her stay with me tonight. Let's face it, the kid's beat'.

'Very well. You will return Charlotte to me by noon tomorrow'.

After a bath and cocoa I got her to bed. I told her what the lawyer said. She was distressed by her technical failure. It was humiliating to think of her mother and step-father finding the bag and raincoat abandoned by the back door, proclaiming her, after all, just a child, unequal to the darkness of the lane.

'But anyway', she said, 'Sib-ay-lee-US. They'll know I mean it now. They said they didn't believe me when I told them I wanted to live with you, but now I've run away'.

'Well, Parcel, we'll need to have a chat and see what's best'. How's that, Mr McLaren, I thought, non-committal enough for the law?

Sunday morning was still wet with a high wind. We both slept in and when breakfast was over it was time to take Charlotte back to her mother's. She was pale, clearly apprehensive, but there were no tears. She held my arm on the bus but without clinging and spoke only to say they'd have to believe her now and look up at me with a resolute 'Sib-ay-lee-US!'

'Well, Charlotte', her mother said, 'I'm very distressed by what you've done and I'm sure Daddy is too'.

I stood with Charlotte facing her in the hall, two errant children taking their row. Charlotte reached for my hand but under the baleful eye dropped her arm and looked at the floor.

'Yes, well, I mean, it was a rotten night', I said. 'She must have felt pretty desperate to go out in it like that'. Dear God, how paltry. Where were the ringing tones of all the fantasy encounters? Silenced by the firm of McLaren, logically and basically.

'I am very sorry that Charlotte felt she wanted to do what she did last night. This is her home and she must settle down in it. I hope we shall have no more of this nonsense, Charlotte'.

'But I told you I want to live with Daddy', Charlotte said, 'And you wouldn't believe me. You're supposed to want me to be happy so you should let me. You should listen to No. 3. Don't you want me to be happy?'

'I think you should go now', her mother said to me, left eyebrow raised.

'No, Daddy, no', Charlotte cried as she ran into my arms. Her mother grabbed her shoulders and pulled. For a second the child spun free, then was back in my arms clamping her body to mine.

'Take me with you, take me with you. I can't stay here. Take me with you'. Then, erect, firing straight at her mother with everything left in her, 'Sib-ay-lee-US!'

'Charlotte, Parcel, listen', I said. 'We're all going to talk about it, what's happened, and we're going to make arrangements that will be best'.

Spent now, she said nothing. I opened the front door and went out to meet the weather she had run through a few hours before. Walking away I lifted my head to take the rain on my face and broke into a run, praying for a stitch in my side as the song she loved came to me in mocking double time. The wind scattered trash from gutters. Tatters of newspaper climbed the wind, showing white against a rain-darkened tenement.

Laces for the lady.

***

212

British universities were jettisoning academic freedom, sinking into management and marketing, government bureaucracy and their own intestinal politics. The Arts were under siege in academe. Scotland was globalizing, becoming smug. There were too many people in suits and twinsets with new Volvos and photographs in *The Scottish Field*. Charlotte had found her independence and was holding her own with the grown-ups. We weren't necessary any more, Sibelius, you and me and No. 3. After fifteen years of Glasgow under the University tower's glowering, Presbyterian surveillance, it was time for pastures new.

Wartime food-parcels from the Mitchells of Ranfurly near Dunedin in the south island of New Zealand arrived regularly to grateful welcomes. Our mutual ancestors had figured in the development of their town. The letters that came with the parcels suggested that New Zealand was a place where a Scot might feel at ease. Then the Ranfurly family visited Glasgow. After dinner one evening the fifteen-year-old daughter stretched, yawned, and said, apparently, 'Well, I'm growing a beard'. Politeness forbade an expression of surprise. We congratulated the young lady on her project and wished her every success. Later we realized that she had said, through her yawn, 'Well, I'm going to bed'. This was an accent, if not a language, to reckon with.

'What's the rest of New Zealand like?' we wondered.

At the art-exhibition opening the man-about-town asked me what I was up to.

'I think I'm going to New Zealand', I said.

The glance he shot me across his flute of *Tio Pepe* was replete with condescension.

'Plucky little country', he said and drifted away in search of someone with ambition.

214

Near Port Jackson, Coromandel

'Have it your way', I thought, 'but it's raining slate pencils outside and I was on the phone today to my prospective employer, the University of Waikato, Hamilton, North Island. The sun's shining down there and the long antipodal summer has just begun'.

I didn't know it, but I was only weeks away from the sub-tropical Coromandel peninsula, its warm Pacific, perfectly laundered breakers and caramel sands, its cosseting February heat, Pohutakawa trees and sleepy motels under a Southern Cross almost touchable in a rush-hour of stars.

A few years later the man-about-town might have lingered in conversation, when New Zealand pluck was Prime Minister David Lange's refusal to admit American nuclear-powered ships into New Zealand waters. No gainsaying the pluck of that message when, as Troy Kennedy Martin's 1985 BBC television mini-series showed us, nuclear-age capitalist cynicism poised Margaret Thatcher's visigothic Britain on the edge of darkness.

An old friend hailed me walking to my office under the unappeasable tower.

'Going to New Zealand? Are you sure you're doing the right thing?' he asked.

'Won't know till I do it'.

'Well, listen', he said, drawing me into the shelter of a doorway, fearful that the forthcoming revelation might be bugged by a stray kiwi in the Glasgow street.

'A friend of ours went to New Zealand. She was there for three months. Through her whole time in the country there was a national shortage of aluminium foil. Think about it'.

I thought about it, packed, and went.

The man-about-town and the friend, were right, up to a point. There was still plenty of pluck to be

216

University of Waikato. The WEL Energy Centre for Performing Arts

found in the vitality of New Zealand's innumerable small businesses and in the developing self-esteem of Maori people; but the 'Think Big' philosophy of Robert 'Piggy' Muldoon's régime was making New Zealand feel less 'little' and increasingly like a would-be mini-America or UK with the multi-nationals calling the shots and corporatization infecting health and education – shades of the Highland Clearances yet again. A once model welfare system was crumbling in the global shift away from socialism. In 1981 the Rugby Union turned deaf ears to the anti-*apartheid* lobby, welcomed a Springbok tour in spite of the insult to New Zealand's non-white people – especially Maori and Pacific Islanders – and split the country. There was an abundance of aluminium foil, but the supermarkets closed at 5 p.m. six days a week. On Saturdays and Sundays even Auckland city, home to a million, nearly a third of the country's population, was a morgue.

Come with me, Sibelius, to Victoria Street, Hamilton's main drag, on a Friday night in the pre-latte 1980s. In those sepia-tinted days the city prefaced total week-end commercial shut-down with a riotous late-night Friday shopping binge when most stores stayed open until the lascivious hour of 9 p.m. While responsible citizens gorged themselves on product, hoons, as I was taught to call them, drove backfiring, supercharged cars and snorting motor bikes up and down Victoria Street shouting at girls and imperilling shoppers' hearing if not their lives, apparently with the connivance of absent police. As a proponent of literature and the arts I wondered how the mild weaponry of poetry, painting and music could possibly avail.

On one such Victoria Street Friday evening, as I contemplated the percentages in an attempt to cross the boiling street, a man turned to me, shrugged.

'Bunch of Yahoos'.

217

218

Victoria Bridge, over the Waikato River, Hamilton

I could have hugged him. Here was Jonathan Swift alive and relevant, thousands of miles from home more than two centuries after his death. I had a new job and for the first time in my life owned a shower. Students were eager. Heating bills were low and avocados cheap. The best was yet to come. At Hamilton's architecturally shameful Founders Theatre Kurt Sanderling made the New Zealand Symphony Orchestra sound like the Dresden Staatskapelle in a performance of Shostakovich's Fifth Symphony; Stephane Grappelli and the Maly Drama Theatre of St Petersburg came to Wellington's International Festival of the Arts; in Auckland Donald MacIntyre sang the title role in The Flying Dutchman; the Soweto String Quartet dropped in for an evening, closely followed by Kathleen Battle, and the New Zealand String Quartet toured the country giving all of Bartók's six quartets on a single day. After I'd presented a programme for Radio New Zealand's classical music Concert station I was overheard speaking to someone at Hamilton's airport. A young man accosted me.

'Didn't I hear you on the radio talking about Sibelius?'

So I didn't have to be a complete outsider in this sporting culture: there were people to talk to even if I was an atheist when it came to rugby.

I shopped for a bed with the lady of my heart. The salesgirl recognized our interest in quality. As I lay testingly on the store's most expensive mattress she turned to my partner and remarked, 'You deserve the beast'.

Growing a beard, deserving the beast? I got the hang of it after a while and learned to appreciate the gifts of a country which offers a compact digest of world landscapes from winterless north, pastoral

219

The Huka River

Waikato and Desert Road to the giant clefts of Fjordland in the south.

There were more bugs than we had in Scotland, mainly flies and cockroaches.

The Yellow Pages crawl with Pest Control experts. I selected Bugbusters, intrigued by the name. They would come tomorrow at 10.00.

Just before 10.00 they called to say their operator was sick. He came the next day.

'Are you better?' I asked.

'Yes, thank you, it must have been a bug'.

Holding my sides I repaired to my office to write the cheque.

'Excuse me', his voice behind me, 'I see you have a picture of Sibelius'.

My writing hand went spastic. A Bugbuster could recognise, even pronounce 'Sibelius'.

'I have all his major works', said Bugbuster, 'and all his piano music. Not many people have the piano music'.

So flies buzzed and cockroaches crawled while Bugbuster and I bonded for ever via the Big Man.

There's Tartan Day and a butcher who specializes in black pudding and haggis. Whisky's about the same price as it is in Glasgow so Colossus from the 'Duke of Argyll' can drop in any time with the assurance that I'll have a bottle and the Second Symphony ready for him. Scotland and Finland merge in this country. I take you to a river in the north island, the Huka. Look, Sibelius, the water's so blue-clean and frothy you can hear the Sixth Symphony. Close by there's a lake, Taupo, to echo your Pielinen or my Loch Lomond. There are pipe bands in every city. There's the south-island village of Glenorchy. It's not far from Queenstown where mountains appropriately called 'The Remarkables' cater to West-of-Scotland

222

Milford Sound, with Mitre peak on the left

Highland nostalgia. There's a shop which imports oatcakes. Robert Louis Stevenson is just up the road, Tusitala home from sea atop Samoa's Mount Vaea.

There are hectares of forest. In 1936 Percy Grainger put up £25 prize money for a composition expressing 'typical New Zealand cultural and emotional characteristics'. Douglas Lilburn thought of his autumn holiday at Peel Forest in South Canterbury. In ten days he wrote his apprentice tone poem, *Forest*, winning the prize with an evocation of wooded shadow, dancing sunlight, mountain moods and pastoral calm. Could he have orchestrated his earth without the tonalities of your *Four Legends from the Kalevala*, Fifth Symphony and *Tapiola*? In his youth New Zealand's premier composer is Lemminkäinen among trees, writing the first of his love letters to nature.

Most of all, on the margin of the world, next stop Antarctica, you can find silence without need of insulating wilderness. The population is more or less four million. That's all, in a country the size of Britain. Fewer people than Finland. There's space. Stay away from the big cities – Auckland, Wellington, Christchurch – and find a house with a bit of land. Apart from spring and summer week-ends when choirs of motorized lawn mowers are likely to disturb the peace, you can listen to the silence (cicadas trill into it in summer) or fill it with music without neighbours complaining as you never could in a Glasgow or Helsinki flat or bungalow. You can make it as loud as you liked to play your records in the wooded seclusion of 'Ainola'. I went 13,000 miles to find the ideal acoustic and bring you into it, Sibelius, with every decibel my transported 'gramophone' could produce. New Zealand's greatest gift was the personal concert hall of my dreams. In my antipodal armchair I could hear every note of the Big Man's music as if for the first time.

Every note was a summons to Finland. Now I must go to see where you were when the music happened. The longship waits on the tarmac, there's a fair wind and a starry sky. Time to head north again, Big Man. Forty years after Mr Adams played *The Swan of Tuonela* in the cold Glasgow music room the pilgrimage begins.

9. Pilgrim

Was there a fellow-addict on the plane from London to Helsinki? Nobody gave a sign but there was one good omen. When I collected Finnish currency from the bank before leaving Britain, there was your face on the hundred-mark notes. Money worries had plagued you for most of your life in spite of the annual pension an enlightened government awarded you in 1897 but, posthumously, you had been co-opted by coin of the realm.

You'd become a major tourist attraction too, judging by the buses continually parked at the monument to you by the sculptor Eila Hiltunen in Helsinki's Sibelius Park. This is my first stop on the way to Koli. You must be pleased with the monument's symbolism, a twenty-four-ton cluster of welded steel tubes, at once an organ, tubular bells, the pipes of a giant Pan, and stalactites of ice. It's backed by trees. To the right of it there's a bust of you, haloed in steel, set in rock. Quite right: nobody's music is more earthed. Maybe the space between your head and the main mass of the monument symbolizes your feeling that your works passed through you into existence from a mystical origin.

'For the most part one is merely a vessel', you wrote to your friend, Axel Carpelan, 'That wonderful logic (let us call it God) which governs a work of art, that is the important thing...It's as if God the Father had thrown down the tiles of a mosaic from heaven's floor and asked me to put them together'.

Tourists from the buses jostle to have their pictures taken beside the monument or touching your sculpted head. But how many of their heads are carrying your sounds? The real marvel is the way the artist has made your sounds visible, especially the combination

225

Sibelius Monument, Helsinki

of rushing surfaces and massive slowness that builds to the final sequence of chords and silences at the end of Symphony No. 5. The monument's gleaming affirmation makes me think of your saying in 1914, 'For an instant God opens his door and His orchestra plays the Fifth Symphony'.

Back on earth, I take a tram to a more fleshly door. One of your favourite Helsinki restaurants is still there, the König, a cellar below street level established in 1892. It became a meeting place for the city's crème de la crème. I ask for your table. You used to sit here for hours with food, wine and cigars in the company of friends including the painter, Akseli Gallen-Kallela and the architect, Eliel Saarinen. Today the management displays a quotation by 'Jean Sibelius, Master Composer':

> *An outsider might think that compositions arise only at the piano. But other things are required: the right atmosphere, old friends, nourishment of mind and body. We discussed the ways of the world and, in passing, the soul did its creative work.*

The next stop is the town of Hämeenlinna on Lake Vanajavesi, a trading place since the 7th century, an hour away from Helsinki. Here your doctor father was in charge of the isolation hospital during the typhus epidemics that came with famine in the 1860s and here's the modest wooden house where he had his surgery and you were born. When the custodian realizes I've come from New Zealand she closes the till: I have proved my *bona fides* by travelling such a long way and there will be no charge for admission. You didn't live in this house for long. When your father died of typhus himself your family was declared

228

The Sibelius Monument from below

bankrupt. There were your mother, your sister Linda and you – and your brother, Christian, was expected soon to complete the musical trio you'd form together later on. Your mother was allowed to keep 'necessary clothes and linen together with two white quilts', and you all moved in with your widowed grandmother.

When you were fourteen you began violin lessons with Hämeenlinna's military bandmaster.

'The violin took me by storm', you said, 'and for the next ten years it was my dearest wish to become a great virtuoso'.

You'd take your violin on country walks and improvise meandering concertos to the birds. These early open-air improvisations are recalled in the *Humoresques* for violin and orchestra and in the first two movements of your Violin Concerto which evoke natural sounds and images – Finnish larks ascending, or the swans and cranes whose voices and being you said affected you more than anything in art, literature or even music. Apart from the question of technique you weren't temperamentally equipped for a soloist's career and suffered badly from stage fright. Yet as late as 1915 when you were composing the *Sonatina* for violin and piano you wrote in your diary, 'Dreamt I was twelve years old and a virtuoso'. In your song, 'The Elf-King' or 'Watersprite', a boy playing his violin beside a waterfall is maddened by the sight of the silver-bearded elf-king. But then we're told that this was only a fantasy of the singer. It's tempting to read your own seduction by the violin into this oddly disturbing poem and your dreams of becoming a virtuoso, but perhaps it's reasonable to hope that with the Concerto you exorcized your youthful ambition.

Around the house of your birth nature has surrendered to dull modern buildings and passing

The entrance to the Birthhouse Museum

traffic, but the house is sensitively maintained as a museum, archive and chamber concert venue. As visitors inspect the exhibits – photographs of Hämeenlinna as it was when you were young, your harmonium, your upright piano and items depicting your rise to international renown – they can listen to recordings of the music of their choice. The custodian apologizes, unnecessarily, when a group of young Koreans requests *Finlandia*, very loud. In the silence after the din of brass and drum and the flutter of Korean hands clapping the voices of Flanagan and Allen croon their perky challenge from the Kilcheran gramophone:

> *Are you havin' any fun?*
> *What y'gettin' out o' livin'?*

Here and now I realize the answer is yes and plenty. Fun was running home from school to tell them I'd just learned your name and heard *The Swan of Tuonela*. Fun was listening to the Second Symphony for the first time with my father and defending Lismore against Douglas's gang of Glasgow Nazis. Fun was waylaying Mr Adams before Prayers to give me back Ex. 19. Fun was watching the First Symphony fill the Great Glen of Scotland. Fun is this, travelling round the world from the cold music room and the back of Ian Whyte's BBC studio to be here, doing obeisance to my jar in Tennessee, paying homage to The Big Man in the place where he began. Fun was dancing to *kwela* music with Margaret on the hard, bare floor of her little waterless house in the Grahamstown location. Thinking of her and the curtained room of the encephalitis time I choose to hear a string quartet. Not the sustaining voices of the profound *Voces Intimae:* it seems more fitting in this house to listen to one of your early works. With Margaret on my mind and the happiness of being

232

here in the first home of The Big Man who made 'pure spring water' a dance seems called for. So I ask for the mazurka-like third movement of your String Quartet in A minor, composed in 1889 when you were twenty-four. If she'd been here, Margaret would have danced again and filled the house with her smile.

**

Half an hour's drive from Helsinki brings me to Järvenpää.

Relishing the buzz of the capital and the company of artistic friends, you'd lived gregariously. You'd travelled to Berlin to study, then to conduct. Paris had applauded the First Symphony at the World Exhibition in 1900; the next year Italy seeded the Second. Now, as you approached your forties you were turning inward, away from the world. You'd had enough of urban Helsinki and wanted country seclusion. There would still be mercurial travels. In 1908 you'd take the Third Symphony to England and in 1914 *The Oceanides* to the USA, but in 1903 you'd bought a plot of land at Järvenpää, 38 kilometres north of Helsinki. Foundations of stone and oak beams were laid for 'Ainola' the chalet-style villa you'd name for your wife, Aino.

'My art demanded a different environment. In Helsinki all melody died within me', you told your friends. 'This home is a necessity for my art. I long to get it all in order'.

So with the newly completed Violin Concerto in your mind you hurry to the house in the woods where you and Aino will live for the rest of your lives.

Yehudi Menuhin remembered a 'cozy wooden house, standing in its own stretch of forest, as must any self-respecting house in Finland'. The house was

233

234

Ainola

designed by Lars Sonck to your specifications in the national Romantic style and built with logs brought from the centre of Finland. You thought it modest.

'The Americans are accustomed to the idea that famous men live like lords', you said. 'They expect to find a castle here, and are very disappointed when they see our little house'.

I doubt the disappointment, Big Man.

Your marriage to Aino sustained you for sixty-five years from early struggles to find your voice to spectacular acclaim in Finland, Britain and America. She saw you through stage-fright, illness, alcoholism, lacerating self-doubt and the thirty-year-long silence when you failed to realize your ambition to compose a crowning symphony superior to the seven you'd made by 1924. Aino knew that you lived in the realm of tone and that the merest fragment of music beyond your mind could sabotage inspiration. No one sang at Ainola; nobody whistled unless you chose otherwise.

During some repairs to the villa a painter liked to whistle while he worked.

'Please don't whistle', requested Aino, 'It bothers the professor'.

The painter looked puzzled.

'Well', said Aino, 'what would you say if someone came along with a broom just when you had finished painting that wall and swept a lot of dirt across it, and ruined the whole job? The professor feels the same way when anyone interrupts his thoughts by whistling'.

The painter understood; the whistling stopped.

'Ainola' is where you brought your family in 1904 and here you died in 1957. You would stand on the porch to greet famous visitors when they appeared round a bend in the pine-lined driveway – Stokowski, Beecham, Flagstad, Ormandy, the President of

Finland. There's the Steinway your friends gave you when you were fifty; there's the laurel wreath Finland gave you when you were eighty-five. Here's the library with your favourite chair in its corner and a galaxy of ash-trays for those world-famous cigars sent to you by Toscanini, Stokowski and Koussevitzky, Vanderbilt and Rockefeller, Fritz Kreisler, Adlai Stevenson, Eisenhower, Marian Anderson, Tallulah Bankhead, Winston Churchill and the Cuban Ministry of Agriculture; here's your radio, though it's probably a later model than the one that brought you Ian Whyte's wartime performance of the Second Symphony; here's the dining room with the table designed by Aino, and the study with your desk, pens and a bed for when you worked late into the night and next morning. A neighbouring farmer's wife was grateful for your midnight oil:

> *He used to work hard right through the*
> *nights and before dawn when we went out to the*
> *cowshed for the morning milking, all the lights*
> *would be on at the Sibelius place. Then when*
> *we'd finished and were on our way back, I'd look*
> *over there and all the lights would be out. He'd*
> *gone to bed, and the house was dark. Sometimes*
> *at night, when I went out to check if the cows*
> *were all right, it would be sort of reassuring*
> *to look that way and see all the lights burning*
> *– someone else besides me was up and working.*

William Carlos Williams knew what was going at the Sibelius place in his poem, 'Tapiola':

Whee-wow! You stayed up half
The night in your attic room under the eves,
*   composing*
secretly, setting it down, period after period,
as the wind whistled. Lightning flashed! The roof

237

Ainola from the garden

creaked about your ears threatening to give
way! But you had a composition to finish that
    could
not wait.

At the back of the house is the grave in a circular clearing among the trees. It's marked by a massive rectangle of stone. Your name is heroic in relief across the centre, and under it, engraved in script, 'Aino Sibelius', the wife who kept you going. On the wreath Aino laid at your funeral the inscription read, 'With gratitude for a life which has been blessed by your great art. Your wife'.

After the First World War you became increasingly reluctant to leave 'Ainola'. Nature surounded you here, and you could watch out for your beloved swans and cranes. 'The swans are always in my thoughts and give splendour to my life', you note in your diary in April 1915. You once told your secretary, Santeri Levas, that the call of the crane was 'the Leitmotiv' of your life. Every spring you waited for the arrival of the migrant birds and everybody in Järvenpää knew that whenever swans or cranes came into sight you were to be told immediately, often by telephone. Among the trees at 'Ainola' it's easy to visualize you as the secluded, introspective artist of *The Bard*, making your own Genesis myth in *Luonnotar*, the tone poem for soprano and orchestra, out of the first poem in the *Kalevala*. Wandering the ocean, heavy with child, the maiden of the air calls for release to Ukko, pagan god of the elements. A scaup or sea-duck panics when it can find no nesting place among the waves. The maiden offers her knee to the duck. There the eggs are laid and break into pieces:

But a wondrous change came o'er them,
And the fragments all grew lovely.

238

From the cracked egg's lower fragment,
Now the solid earth was fashioned,
From the cracked egg's upper fragment,
Rose the lofty arch of heaven,
From the yolk, the upper portion,
Now became the sun's bright lustre;
From the white, the upper portion,
Rose the moon that shines so brightly;
Whatever in the egg was mottled,
Now became the stars in heaven,
Whatever in the egg was blackish,
In the air as clouds now floated.

The maiden gives birth to Väinämöinen, the culture hero who sings the world to wonder or ecstatic dance. The formidable two-octave tessitura of the vocal part – human power stretched to the limit – conveys the intensity of the act of creation, while the orchestral writing expresses its definitive beauty. The work is a metaphor for your own process of composition.

'Ainola' is where you conceived or composed all your major works from the Third Symphony on. And this is where you tried to compose an Eighth Symphony which would carry your art beyond even the uniquely compact majesty of the Seventh. The new work vexed you for nearly thirty years, though there were surely times of exhilaration too, when you could hear it finished in your imagination and when you sent the first movement to the copyist. The world waited, and you promised American and British premières to Koussevitzky and Basil Cameron. But in 1945 you told Santeri Levas that you had destroyed the symphony.

'My Eighth Symphony', you said, 'has already been "ready" – "ready" in inverted commas – several times. I even went so far as to put it in the fire'.

So we waited in vain. The evidence is that you composed the symphony, but didn't think it good enough.

'Heaven on earth begins', you said, 'when a man forsakes self-criticism'. But after your death Joonas Kokkonen identified an organ piece called *Surusoitto*, or 'Funeral Music', which you contributed to the funeral service for Gallen-Kallela, as probably derived from the score of the Eighth Symphony, and Aino agreed with Kokkonen. If this is as close as we can get to the work that was not to be, perhaps we can draw our own comfort and assume yours from the untroubled character of the piece. It's tranquil, lyrical and strong.

240

The grave at Ainola

10. Koli

My last stop is Koli. The green monotony of trees on the journey from Helsinki takes away any sense of being about to arrive anywhere, but suddenly the bus pulls into a square. This is Ukkokoli, close to the summit of Koli Mountain with a view of Lake Pielinen below, gleaming in the immaculate light of the short Finnish summer. A chair-lift goes down to the lakeside. There are giant rocks down there and enticing coves. The woods along the lakeside are silent, even lacking birdsong, but big dragonflies whirr like helicopters on a mission, accentuating the peace. The sky is clear, pale blue, but the quietness recalls your struggle with what you called 'the dreadful overtones of eternal stillness'. Were you remembering Pascal's famous admission: 'Le silence éternel des espaces infinis m'effraie' ('The eternal silence of these infinite spaces terrifies me')? Perhaps all your symphonies are interrogations of silence. Full of islands, the lake sends its shining up to the mountain. It's a stage set for the mythical tales of the *Kalevala*.

Here you would have understood Elgar's saying that 'music is in the air all around us'; all you had to do was 'take as much as you require'. Horns call across the watery spaces, strings sing in the firs, brass and percussion declaim from the rocks. It's the *Karelia Suite*, *Spring Song* and *The Dryad*. There's gallant Björn, hunter of *The Wood Nymph*, riding into goblins, moonbeams and the doom of love that waits for him in the forest: 'The heart that is stolen by a wood-nymph is never returned'. It's the birthplace of Symphony No. 4, which Otto Klemperer called 'the solitary song of a man who does not care for loud success'. It's your music made visible.

You went to Koli at the end of September 1909 with your brother-in-law, Eero Järnefelt. While Järnefelt

241

painted you wandered in the forests and took sustenance from the splendour of the great lake and its innumerable tree-clad islands. Seventeen years earlier you'd spent your honeymoon with Aino on the other side of the lake. Now you reflected on your marriage, your seemingly endless financial problems and your recent fear of early death until the tumour in your throat had been removed. Now that the fear was over you could deal with the emotion it had generated. The majesty of Finland's most spectacular scenery inspired you to develop ideas for a piece to be called 'The Mountain'. By the following January you'd incorporated these ideas into your plan for the Fourth Symphony.

What else were you feeling while the Fourth was beginning to take shape? Are there clues in other music you were making at the same time? Soon after your return from Koli you composed two Shakespeare songs for a production of *Twelfth Night*. In 'Come away, death' unrequited love consigns the lover to a black coffin in an unmarked grave. Did the 'fair, cruel maid' of the song become the whispers and briefly whirling waltz of your elusive tree-nymph in *The Dryad*, the most compact of your symphonic poems, composed in February 1910? The transience of life occupied you again in Shakespeare's 'When that I was and a little tiny boy'. You worked on *In Memoriam*, a 'Funeral March for Orchestra'. The scoring is Mahlerian but the precedent is Siegfried's Funeral March in *Götterdämmerung*. You wanted it to be 'on the grandest scale'. When the proofs came from Breitkopf und Härtel you immediately decided to 'rescore it, every bar!' and it occupied you until the following March, so you clearly attached great emotional significance to the piece.

'It's strange to think of it', you mused in your diary, 'but I suppose it will be played when I am buried'.

Lake Pielinen from Koli Mountain

Then the world went dark. You were revising the 1902 score of your cantata, *The Origin of Fire* with a text from Rune 47 of the *Kalevala*. Louhi, Mistress of Pohjola has hidden the sun and moon. Finland's Thor, the great god Ukko, kindles flame from his sword. He gives it to the maiden of the air to nurse so that a new sun and moon may be fashioned from the brightness. The maiden rocks the flame in a golden cradle but then lets it drop. The fire cleaves the sky, falling to earth – and there you end the story. Why not go on to tell how old Väinämöinen and the eternal smith, Ilmarinen, search for the fire, learning of the devastation it has brought to the Kalevalanders? A house is destroyed, a baby burned in its cradle. A lake boils over its embankments. The fire is swallowed by a fish, and that fish is swallowed by another and then another. Väinämöinen catches the last fish, cuts it open and takes a spark of fire from the belly of the first fish to light up the dark houses while Ilmarinen quenches the destructive flames. Why didn't you make music from all this? What's wrong with a happy ending? Why did you end the cantata where you did, giving us only a narrative torso when you had such rich material to draw on? Or does the music itself imply an answer? It's compellingly Sibelian when you're evoking darkness, but perfunctory when you're telling us about the maiden of the air and the fate of the fire when it slips from her fingers. It wasn't the restoration of light but the darkness itself that commanded your imagination. Might you have seen profound mythological potential in the rest of the story after the fire-storms of Dresden, the nuclear cauldrons of Hiroshima and Nagasaki and the twenty-first century's fear of nuclear proliferation?

You also revised *Rakastava*, 'The Lover', making it your most exquisite work for string orchestra. First composed in 1893 for male voice choir, you amplified it with a string accompaniment the following year, then rearranged it in 1898 for mixed choir *a capella*. In 1911 you prepared its last incarnation in the version we usually hear for strings, triangle and timpani. If the *a capella* version is winsome, the final version is all delicacy and yearning. It shows how much more you can say when you're working with an orchestral palette, however limited. The winged feet of the ardent lover scarcely touch the ground in the *perpetuum mobile* of the central movement, 'The Path of the Beloved', but even here love goes together with loss. 'Where are you, my own beloved?' asks the lover in the words of the *Kanteletar* for the first movement. 'Here my darling has walked', begins the second movement, implying that she's not there for him now. In the last movement he entreats a hand, an embrace, a kiss and bids her farewell as once again his dryad fades beyond his reach.

Well yes, of course, Sibelius; for me, as you'd realize, it's Margaret music. Eventually South African poet and singer Vusi Mahlasela would bring the tender consolation of his song, 'Sleep Tight, Margaret', from the music of his country's reconstruction. It was as if he knew the story of that shattering day in Grahamstown.

Sleep tight Margaret
Girl don't you worry
You will always come against the tide
Some days are golden
And some are just stones
Let the bed and the pillow comfort your cries
Like a cloud
Carry you to a new day
New day, new life
Releasing the misfortunes
that carried us through yesterday

So while I'm remembering the loss of Margaret I'm also thinking about you developing the Fourth Symphony in your mind, much possessed by death, darkness, loneliness, love and loss. You felt alienated from the world as you often did, even when you had moved beyond the Fourth Symphony and were sketching ideas for the Fifth and Sixth.

'Am alone, alone, and again alone!' you wrote in your diary on 7 December 1914, 'We all live together in our home country and manage to get on famously. Yet underneath it all we hate each other good and proper'.

Again, on 17 December: 'Only solitude. I alone, alone, alone!'

Probably the clearest indication of your prevailing mood during the gestation of the Fourth is your setting of Runeberg's 'Idle Wishes' in the songs of Opus 61:

> *Waves without number wander*
> *the face of the glittering sea.*
> *If only I could be*
> *one ocean billow among many,*
> *indifferent to the depths of my being,*
> *carefree and chill and clear,*
> *without a single memory*
> *of happier days gone by!*

If the sea is cold and indifferent, so are the people around you:

> *Here too I go among*
> *a host of cold waves –*
> *they play with joy and pain,*
> *they smile and weep in jest,*
> *only I have my burning heart –*
> *if only like them I lacked one!*

And even if you could be a wave in the sea you 'would be no different from now', you couldn't be 'carefree and chill and clear' like the others. You'd still be burdened with the heart's vulnerabilities, your sense of isolation, your capacity for anguish and the big, difficult questions. Runeberg's poem might stand as epigraph for the Fourth Symphony, the music in which you most comprehensively register the changing moods of a nature eternally heedless of the human heart yet always affecting it.

There were more of the endemic financial crises requiring stressful visits to bankers in Helsinki. After much labour you abandoned work on a commission to write an orchestral song for the great dramatic soprano, Aino Ackté, based on Edgar Allan Poe's 'The Raven'. At last, after the further distractions of conducting engagements in Gothenburg and Riga, you went home to 'Ainola' and your long-suffering Aino to focus on the Symphony.

Nobody clapped at the end of the first performance on 3rd April 1911 until the usual bouquets were brought onstage signalling the end of the music. Critics were as baffled as the concert-goers.

'Everything seems strange', wrote one Finnish commentator. 'Curious, transparent figures float here and there, speaking to us in a language whose meaning we cannot grasp. Posterity must decide whether the composer has overstepped the boundaries dictated by sound, natural musicianship'.

American critics in New York and Boston weren't inclined to wait for posterity.

'It sounds like the improvisation of an unskilled organist...There are sounds and lamentations in the air, that is, if there were any air, which there is not, for mere tune is left out of this miscalled symphony.

There were dissonant and doleful mutterings, generally leading nowhere... It is a composition which the earnest music-lover will "first endure" and "then pity", but never embrace... His Fourth Symphony is a dismal failure'.

But not for Delius who heard you conduct the first British performance in October 1912 at the Birmingham Festival. The concert also premièred Elgar's new Ode, *The Music Makers*.

'Elgar's work is not very interesting', Delius wrote to his wife, Jelka, 'and very noisy. It did not interest me. Sibelius interested me much more – He is trying to do something new & has a fine feeling for nature & he is also unconventional'.

In Herbert von Karajan's opinion the Fourth is 'one of the few symphonies – like Brahms's Fourth and Mahler's Sixth – that ends in disaster'. Well, maybe, though it's a questionable reading of the ingenuity with which Brahms's variations in his last movement lay out a conspectus of moods and states of mind before accelerating into a full-blooded finale of absolute conviction. Otto Klemperer felt that your Fourth 'ends in complete darkness'. But the Scottish poet, Hugh MacDiarmid, got it right when he called it your 'gaunt El-Greco-emaciated ecstatic Fourth'. It's the Romantic ecstasy of the confessional combined with the aesthetic ecstasy of rigorous control.

'Don't lose the sense of life's pain and pathos', you told yourself in a diary entry while composing it, 'All my youth and childhood, the corpses still rise to the surface. Help!'

Reviewing 'the best performance that London has ever heard' of the Fourth Symphony under Beecham at the Queen's Hall in December 1937 EMI's Walter Legge, who would become talent scout supreme in the world of classical music, wrote that the Symphony 'is the limit even he has reached in sparseness…The few who left the hall at the end must have been surprised to see that there is still active life on this planet'. On one of his visits to 'Ainola' Legge asked you why you hadn't continued in the same vein as the Fourth.

'Beyond that', you replied, 'lies madness or chaos'.

But there's no self-indulgence, no wallowing. As you said, there's 'nothing, absolutely nothing of the circus about it'. Cecil Gray, among the first in Britain to understand your music, called the symphony a 'White Dwarf', not because he thought it like a star low in luminosity but like one in which matter is highly compressed. Yet for all its bony structure and chamber-music restraint the Fourth is your most all-embracing symphony. Barring the satirical, every human mood can be heard in it as well as the range of nature's changing faces.

There's a growl in the lower strings and bassoons. The beginning, you said, should sound 'as harsh as fate'. The great lake is black under a lowering winter sky. The firs are ghostly skeletons behind drifting veils of mist. Hard rain whips the granite shores. Thematic motives erupt and drop into abysses. A sombre cello solo leads to a precarious serenity which is shattered by brass before an anguished soliloquy. Light cuts briefly across the black water in the second movement's *allegro vivace*, but is enveloped in wraiths of woodwind in the third movement. The last movement begins vigorously, determined to be spirited. A glockenspiel dances, flickerings of eerie light in the firs, but darkness supervenes. In a desolate coda the music falters. After a cry of flutes and oboes, it dies. We are left poised between desolation and stoic resignation, or, as your friend Rosa Newmarch said, 'alone with nature's breathings'. Alone, most of all, with you.

Your music is not merely the Finnish landscape, of course, but it contains it and is fed by it. The correlation between what is seen and what is heard will always be mysterious. Yet, from these northern distances, from the forests, the islands, and the waters of your country you bring the sound of inscrutably regenerative nature. In Marcel Proust's phrase, 'never was spoken language so inexorably determined'. But the language of your music still maintains itself between contradictions. I think you'd have got on well with Hugh MacDiarmid. Like you he took his stand on the isthmus of the middle state:

I'll ha'e nae hauf-way hoose, but aye be whaur
Extremes meet – it's the only way I ken
To dodge the curst conceit o' bein richt
That damns the vast majority o' men.

The conclusion of the Seventh is a place where extremes meet, as equivocal as the titanic chords that end the Fifth. Perhaps you'd have agreed with Dencombe, the ageing author of Henry James's 'The Middle Years'. Like you he is 'a passionate corrector, a fingerer of style':

> *We work in the dark – we do what we can – we*
> *give what we have. Our doubt is our passion and*
> *our passion is our task. The rest is the madness*
> *of art.*

Long before the Seventh was finished you described its projected character: 'The VII Symphony. Joy of life and vitality, with *appassionato* passages'. Planning came readily enough; composition was tough going. There were nights of anguished struggle with your material when you despaired and drank heavily for courage to go on.

250 'How dreadful old age is for a composer', you

wrote in your diary, 'Things don't go as quickly as they used to, and self-criticism grows to impossible proportions'.

Not impossible after all, Big Man, as the finished masterpiece proves. The music climbs up from darkness as if emerging from the unconscious, a creature rising from primordial mud or perhaps your own creativity heaving itself up from crippling self-criticism. It moves slowly towards the pervasive radiance of an all-important trombone theme, just over 11 minutes into the score. We might think of Jean Anouilh's description of tragedy: 'The spring is wound up tight. It will uncoil of itself'. So your music uncoils through fluent episodes of search and repose, affirmation and uncertainty. There's always a sense of forward movement, what you called 'the compelling vein that goes through the whole', but the simultaneous use of contrary tempi solidifies the Symphony into a sculpture fixed in space, aloof from linear time, a suspended block of ever-present passion and philosophy. When the music stops on the precipice of its C major cadence it's like the crest of a great wave that must remain colossally frozen until it breaks on the primal darkness from which the Symphony grows and will then grow again in an eternal return to the perplexities of the human condition. The Symphony endorses George Steiner's apothegm: 'Structure is itself interpretation'.

In 1925, the year after the première of the Seventh, consciously or not, you gave us your own comment on the precipice of its ending. Melodrama in the form of recitation to musical accompaniment was outmoded by the early twentieth century, but you chose this genre for the short work for voice and piano you called 'A Lonely Ski-trail'. The Swedish text is by your friend, Bertel Gripenberg, who died in

1947. No doubt your revision of the piece as late as 1948 was intended partly as homage to Gripenberg, but the elegiac character of the new accompaniment for strings and harp, the imagery of the text and your decision to resuscitate the piece so far into the silence from Järvenpää encourage us to hear in it a consummating statement, perhaps your last confession of faith before, like Prospero in *The Tempest*, you'd break your staff and drown your book. You feel your thoughts 'slipping further and further away'. The ski-trail is life and it's lonely:

> *A lonely ski-trail that disappears*
> *In the loneliness of the forest,*
> *A human life that runs itself out*
> *On paths that no one knows.*

The trail ends at a 'sudden precipice'. Snow-flakes cover the tracks.

It's a fitting metaphor for many lives, but not for yours, Sibelius. Plenty of snow has fallen since your death on 20th September 1957, but it hasn't hidden your tracks. They've brought many to Koli and remain fresh and beckoning for anyone who cares to see and hear. When you first wrote the piece in 1925 you were standing on the high edge where the Seventh Symphony ends, looking out towards the frigid epicentre of *Tapiola*. You're there still.

The progression of seamless organic transformations in the Seventh Symphony rises, certainly, to a majestic climax; there's vitality all right and there are intimations of joy along the way, but isn't it finally the majesty of a consciousness that knows both ecstasy and anguish, facing the unknowable, the possibility of a void? Did you know you were composing a parable about our rite of passage across what Vladimir Nabokov calls 'the crack of light between two eternities of darkness', the music unfolding a paraphrase of our lives from the prenatal abyss of its beginning to its final prospect of impersonal timelessness? It's the great paradox of music that an art which shapes itself in time can lift us above it. Significant form endows a work with a transcendental quality and it was Gustav Holst's feeling for transcendence that enabled him to make one of the most gnomic pronouncements about the nature of music: 'Music, being identical with heaven, isn't a thing of momentary thrills, or even hourly ones. It's a condition of eternity'.

Like all great art your music registers our intuition that a narrow material world, unlit by imagination, is inadequate to human experience. Refining consciousness is your job, intensifying and enhancing it. You know about conflict, exaltation, perplexity, triumph, defeat and resignation. You are at once distinctive and transparent, an Aeolian harp breathing universal propositions that make a myth not of gods and heroes but of the soul itself. As part of nature you are part of us. If your vision is finally a tragic one, you know that this is compatible with the fact of human hope, just as W. B. Yeats, who also learned from swans about the eternal and the transient, could write of gaiety transfiguring dread in the tragedies of *Hamlet* and *King Lear*. Like all great artists you are engaged with the doubleness of life. So, in the music for the play *Everyman* by von Hofmannsthal, Everyman invites his friends to a party. There will be a banquet, dancing and love as certainly as your tune is catchy and charming; but the rhythm isn't tipsy enough to be convincingly Bacchanalian and Everyman has seen the approach of Death.

'There is always this element of ambivalence in Sibelius's music', says the Finnish conductor, Osmo

Vänskä, 'as though the music sounds "through the tears". There is always this kind of shadow. Maybe it's a Finnish thing'.

Everyman's song is bittersweet: it's that ambivalence again from an artist driven by the compulsion to say what is ultimately and for ever right. It's often said of an artist that he came at a difficult time. How do you write an epic if you're a poet born after Milton? It took a Wordsworth. How do you follow Mozart? You become Beethoven. How do you compose in the immediate aftermath of *Tristan und Isolde?* You are Mahler. How do you produce integrated symphonic forms after Brahms? You are Sibelius. Schoenberg said he believed that you had the breath of a true symphonist. His idea of art defines your life-long enterprise:

> *Art is a cry of distress from those who live out*
> *within themselves the destiny of humanity, who*
> *are not content with it but measure themselves*
> *against it, who do not obtusely serve the engine*
> *to which the label 'unseen forces' is applied,*
> *but throw themselves into the moving gears to*
> *understand how it works…Inside them turns the*
> *movement of the world; only an echo of it leaks*
> *out — the work of art.*

In Finland you could never be doomed Kullervo who couldn't get the knack of things. You will always be steady old Väinämöinen, the eternal singer, living your times. Everywhere you're Charlotte's 'Sib-ay-lee-US', singing for us all. A Scot might think of you as the MacCrimmon piper in the Gaelic poet, Sorley MacLean's 'The Cave of Gold', where music is a mystical ordering power. Like the MacCrimmon you were often bewildered, close to losing your way. Like him you carried on:

254

.... as he went on in his perplexity
with no struggle but the plea of the music,
he did not let go his pipe.
The sword was useless,
it was the music strengthened his step,
it was the music itself that strove.
The pipe itself had the power...

its genesis, purpose and meaning,
the argument that was in its cry,
though weak yet stronger than the strongest
hero ever seen on field
wrestling with the green bitch of death.

Here on Koli Mountain, your Bàrr Mòr, with its radiant show of the numinous, impersonal nature which can annihilate us or bring us an unequalled source of consolation and joy, the Seventh Symphony sings with the ultimate nobility of the grand Perhaps. 'We must try to love so well the world that we may believe, in the end, in God', says Robert Penn Warren. Up here it might be possible. Even at this altitude the summer afternoon is warm and still. In the gentle sunshine tenacious mountain shrubs glisten among the grey rocks, a shimmer of praise in Harris-tweed green. Faint but unmistakable, there's a smell of mixed herbs. I'll wait on my rock for the sunset touch.

It's journey's end for a junky. I am so grateful to have travelled here from the cold Scottish music room of my youth. Grateful beyond speech, except to say at last, thank you, Big Man.

London, 1997; talking to Sir Colin Davis

10 October 1997

My instructions from Sir Colin's agent are to arrive 7 Highbury Terrace, London N5 promptly at 10 a.m. and to leave at 11 sharp. I arrive early by ten minutes on a sunny autumn morning, so sit on a bench in Highbury Fields conning my preparatory notes. The main topic of conversation will be the music of Sibelius. At precisely 10 a.m. I stand at the front door, which is open, and ring the bell. A woman is standing on the stairs at the far end of the hallway, presumably Lady Davis. 'Please come in', she says, pointing further up to where the staircase bends out of sight. 'I think you'll find the man you're looking for waiting for you up here'. I climb the stairs and round the bend. Sir Colin looks down at me, smiling. I say, 'Hello, Sir Colin. It's very good of you to see me'. We shake hands and he says, 'Thank you for coming'. He takes me into a bright, creamy sitting room with piles of scores lying around. I'm given an easy chair at right angles but close to the couch on which he sits at my end.

MW: It's a long time since I sat at the back of Studio 1 at the Glasgow BBC listening to you conducting Ian Whyte's BBC Scottish Orchestra.

CD: It's a very long time — about 40 years ago. Where did they go?

MW: If we talk about that there won't be any time left to talk about Sibelius.

CD: That *is* Sibelius.

257

MW: You recorded all the Sibelius symphonies with the Boston Symphony Orchestra in the 1970s. Now you've just finished recording your second cycle with the London Symphony Orchestra.

CD. Yes. We've just done the Seventh along with *Kullervo* — the first and the last together. I'd give you a copy but I haven't got it yet, so I don't know if they're any good.

MW: Why do you think you have this affinity with Sibelius?

CD: I don't know. Who can know the answer to such a question? Why do *you* have the affinity? What does he mean to you?

MW: That's the mystery I'm trying to understand. Maybe it's the stage I was at in life when I heard him first. I was a boy ready for music and he went in deep because I got him early. Maybe it's a northern feeling, a Finn speaking to a Scot. Maybe it's the palette. What is the palette? Maybe it's the vigorous, even joyous acceptance of tragedy.

CD: The palette is low — lots of low flutes, and pedal point. Of *course* it's tragic. The beginning of the Seventh is something — some 'rough beast' — climbing up out of the mud towards you. (I can't help quoting Yeats when I talk about this *[Sir Colin is quoting from W. B. Yeats's poem, 'The Second Coming']*)...The symphony is about death. He confronts it. This dark throb is there even in the slow movement of the Third Symphony, my favourite when I was a kid. It's all in the way he puts the pieces together — like life — making it cohere. Then, like life, it's over. And there's lots of space. Sibelius needs space. He's heroic, a wild, emotional man. Music is above all about emotions.

MW: What do you think of Paavo Berglund's insistence that Sibelius's symphonies are pure music?

CD: There's no such thing as pure music. Well, there is, but I don't like it!

MW: In the old days in Glasgow you used to play Stravinsky. I particularly remember performances of the *Symphony in Three Movements*.

CD: Yes, I used to like that very much. But I don't want to do Stravinsky now — it's so balletic.

MW: When Sibelius finds a theme he always has to break from it. It's surely not just an updating of sonata form's development section. It's something else emotionally and psychologically, I think. It's a drama in which he has to risk departing from security, as if his luck in finding the tune has been too good to be true and has to be tested to see if it'll hold. He has to set out to earn his way back to the theme, find his way back at a deeper level. Do you think that's right?

CD: Yes, that's right. He has to take it apart and put the pieces together again. That's the story. And there's *always* a story. Compare the second movement of the Third Symphony to the second movement of Beethoven's opus 59 no. 3. It's a song and a story.

MW: This is especially true in the Second

Symphony. The beginning of the Symphony is like an accompaniment which is searching for something to accompany, looking for a partner.

CD: That's right. It's part of a sexual scheme of things. And it's masculine. In the last movement of the Second, after the first statement of the theme he uses in the conclusion, after that tune he goes into a cathedral. He gets thrown out, but he gets back, like Parsifal. Sibelius's music is very male — a woman couldn't have written it.

MW: My visit in Finland to the northern Karelia convinced me that there's a connection between his music and landscape. I felt the same sort of connection in Arnold Bax on a recent visit to his favourite village in north-west Donegal. Berglund denies this connection in Sibelius when he insists that the symphonies are pure music.

CD: Landscape, yes, but it's any landscape *[looks out of window towards Highbury Fields]* — like that. A beautiful late summer day, falling leaves in sunlight. Soon it will all be over again. Oh, Berglund's wrong. *[In the window stands an apparently human skeleton covered by a sheet, but a bony foot remains exposed.]*

MW: My God, look at that foot!

CD: Please do!

MW: Quite a *memento mori*. Can we please go back to landscape for a moment?

CD: Sibelius is full of nature. It's seductive and terrifying: children playing, naked girls, the horns

260

of elfland, frightening things in the dappled woods, teasing, alluring, terrifying. This is the world of the 6th Symphony. The opening of that symphony is utterly beautiful — nothing is more beautiful. But we can't know, we can hardly imagine what it must have felt like to be him any more than we can imagine what it must have felt like to be Mozart. What *can* it have been like to possess a complete intellectual apparatus, to be able to do anything? Mozart was like that. Or think of Berlioz.

MW: You remember the story of Sibelius's meeting with Mahler in 1907 when Sibelius said he admired the symphony's logic and severity of form and Mahler said no, the symphony must contain everything, must be like the world. But it seems to me that Sibelius combines severity of form with inclusiveness. The Fourth Symphony is cryptic and severe, but includes a full spectrum of human moods. It seems to me that Sibelius's music is talking at a deeper level than Mahler's.

CD: Absolutely. Sibelius is so *big* — and much deeper than Mahler who's so prolix... Mahler is just reportage. I can't bear that 5th Symphony, but I know I mustn't say that! Mahler didn't know when to stop. Sibelius didn't know how to begin!

MW. I suppose that becomes sadly true with the Eighth Symphony which we'll never hear. Do you know the organ piece *Surusoitto*, or 'Funeral Music' which Joonas Kokkonen tells us is derived from the score of the Eighth?

CD. No, I'm sorry. I don't know that piece. But what was left to write after the Seventh? He'd done

261

it.

MW: It's nearly 11 o'clock, so I think I must release you now as per instruction.

CD: Not at all. Plenty of time. You've got another five minutes.

MW: Well, I must leave Sibelius and set off to Worcester in pursuit of Elgar now. Have you ever followed his trail?

CD: No, I've never done that. I like Elgar very much. He's so gloomy [smiling broadly]. It's so irrational to be cheerful!

I leave promptly. He sees me to the door. 'If you do write a book about all this', he says, 'let me know and I'll buy it'. I say, 'I'll try'. We shake hands and he says, 'Best wishes'.

P. S.

It takes nerve to write to an immortal.

'Who do you think you are? Don't be ridiculous. How could he possibly be interested in anything you might have to say, you down there?'

Even compulsive gratitude might have quailed without encouragement from sympathetic friends.

'Go ahead. You must. Tell him how you feel, what a companion he's been. He won't mind. He'll be glad to hear from you'.

So thanks especially to Tim Dodd, peerless producer of classical music features for Radio New Zealand Concert, who saw in some of the Letter a potential for radio programmes, and to Jan Pilditch who always believed others might like to share the stories. I'm grateful to the editors of *London Magazine*, *P.N. Review* and *The Drouth* for thinking earlier incarnations of some of these ideas fit to print.

For conversation, fellow-feeling and argument, thanks to Joy Aberdein, Lucy Alcock, Ken Arvidson, Ralph Bartlett, Patrick and Pam Beehan, Jillene Bydder, John Cairney, David Campbell, Tim Couzens, Winnie Crombie, Sir Colin Davis, Penelope Dunkley, Ritva Eskola, David Fine, David Foreman, Michael Goodson, Guy Grant, Paul Griffiths, Rodney Hamel, Janice Hamilton, Peter and Lucienne Hunter, Di Johnson, Harold Kidd and son, Michael and Colleen Lascelles, Robert Layton, Eric and Sheila Liggett, Martin Lodge, Fabio Lucas, James McCall, Hugh Macdonald, Alan and Sheila Park, Julie Posa, Hugh C. Rae, Alan Riach, John Rocchiccioli, Kit Rollings, Peter and Rosemary Scott, Warwick and Jan Silvester, John Smart, Grahame Smith, Lygia Fagundes Telles, Sam Tennyson, Erwin Theodor, Osmo Vänskä, Elsie

Walker, Maria Walker, Guyon and Sonia Wells, Willie Winton.

English speakers who wish to know Sibelius must be as indebted as I am to Erik Tawaststjerna's monumental study of the composer in its three-volume English translation by Robert Layton (Faber, 1976-97). Layton's own 'Master Musicians' guide to the composer (fourth edition, Dent, 1992) remains invaluable, a model book of its kind. Benefiting from information that has come to light in recent years, Andrew Barnett's *Sibelius* (Yale University Press, 2007) is a comprehensive and engaging biography by a learned and perceptive Sibelian familiar to many through his CD liner notes for recordings of Sibelius's music by BIS.

The quotation in Letter 4 from Book 1, Chapter 15 of William McIlvanney's novel, *Docherty* (1975), appears by kind permission of the author. Thanks to William Farrimond, COD Department of Humanities, University of Waikato for financial assistance with scanning. Photographs of the Elliot Junction rail disaster are reproduced by courtesy of the Angus Council, Angus Cultural Services. The photograph of Ian Whyte is kindly supplied by the BBC Scottish Symphony Orchestra.

Some names have been changed to protect the innocent, the guilty and the writer.

264

Index

273

The writer at Sibelius's table, the Konig, Helsinki

Printed in the United States
146683LV00005B/85/P